杭州社会资源
国际旅游访问点导览

A Guide to Hangzhou Social Resources
International Tourism Visiting Places

李晓红 著

ZHEJIANG UNIVERSITY PRESS
浙江大学出版社

图书在版编目（CIP）数据

杭州社会资源国际旅游访问点导览 ＝A Guide to
Hangzhou Social Resources International Tourism
Visiting Places:汉英对照 / 李晓红著. -- 杭州：
浙江大学出版社，2019.12
　　ISBN 978-7-308-19781-6

　　Ⅰ.杭… Ⅱ.①李… Ⅲ.①社会组织-介绍-杭州
-汉、英 Ⅳ.①C232.551

中国版本图书馆CIP数据核字（2019）第275568号

杭州社会资源国际旅游访问点导览

李晓红　著

责任编辑　周群
责任校对　虞雪芬　宁　檬
封面设计　海　海
出版发行　浙江大学出版社
　　　　　（杭州市天目山路148号　邮政编码310007）
　　　　　（网址：http：//www.zjupress.com）
排　　版　杭州隆盛图文制作有限公司
印　　刷　虎彩印艺股份有限公司
开　　本　710 mm×1000 mm　1/16
印　　张　14.75
字　　数　285千
版 印 次　2019年12月第1版　2019年12月第1次印刷
书　　号　ISBN 978-7-308-19781-6
定　　价　59.00元

前　言

2017，杭州成功入选联合国世界旅游组织（UNWTO）全球旅游最佳实践样本城市。杭州样本的优点和突出表现之一就是在全国率先推出社会资源国际旅游访问点项目。该项目寻找国际游客眼里最独特的"杭州生活"，让国际游客通过深度体验了解杭州、爱上杭州，是将社会资源转化为旅游产品的重要举措，凸显了杭州旅游"主客共享"的独特品质，推动了杭州旅游的国际化和全域化。

截至目前，杭州共有社会资源国际旅游访问点130余个，涵盖城市公共服务、工业旅游、农业旅游、社会生活、社会政治及市民生活六大类。而2017年推出的全国首个访问点领域的地方标准《社会资源国际旅游访问点设置与服务规范》（DB 3301/T0208-2017），更是规范了访问点管理工作，提升了访问点的服务品质。

一个个访问点就是藏在杭州美景中的一颗颗珍珠。本书精选22个访问点，图文并茂，中英对照，系统全面地介绍杭州社会资源国际旅游访问点，将颗颗珍珠串联在一起，让全世界感受更真实的杭州风情。此书也尝试将文化与旅游结合起来，讲述访问点中的文化故事。

杭州市旅游形象推广中心（杭州市商务会展旅游促进中心）为本书的编撰牵线搭桥，提供了大力支持。相关访问点也提供了丰富的素材。浙江省中国国际旅行社资深导游孙艺实地走访了各访问点并对访问点的中文稿做了梳理和提炼工作，浙江旅游职业学院的佘雄飞老师完成了杭州都锦生实业有限公司、杭州市富阳中医骨伤医院、东山农贸市场的英文译稿，陈玥老师完成了杭州王星记扇业有限公司、杭州万事利丝绸文化博物馆、杭州萧山南宋官窑艺术馆的英文译稿，徐劼成老师完成了清河坊历史文化街区和康师傅梦想探索乐园的英文译稿。此外，浙江旅游职业学院的丁方、曾祥程和杨晓雯老师为访问点的英文翻译提供了帮助，在此一并致谢。

李晓红

2019 年 4 月 8 日

目 录

三、社会文化

Contents

1 Public Services

2 Industrial Tourism

3 Social Culture

城市公共服务

City Public Services

清河坊历史文化街区

清河坊历史文化街区是杭州市区唯一的、仍完整地保持着古城历史风貌的老街，并被国家旅游局评为 AAAA 级景区。名人、老巷、旧居、老店在这里交相辉映，它在杭州的城市文化中扮演了非常重要的角色。

杭州市区有十几条特色街区，其中清河坊历史文化街区最为有名。它位于杭州市上城区吴山北麓，毗邻西湖风景区，东起江城路，西至南山路，全长 1800 米，宽 13 米，整个街区占地面积 13.66 公顷。南宋时这一带是都城杭州的"皇城根儿"，它紧临赵构皇帝的德寿宫和御街。清朝期间其又是王权中心，不少官署衙门都驻扎在此，因此河坊街一带许多小巷的名称都与官衙有关。清末民初，河坊街一带商铺云集。这里的各类店铺约有一百余家，如胡庆余堂、方裕和南北货店、边福茂鞋店、邵芝岩笔庄等。河坊街与中山中路的交叉口当时称"四拐角"，这里分别被孔凤春香粉店、宓大昌烟店、万隆火腿店、张允升帽庄四个著名店家各踞一角，成为远近闻名的商业中心。当时闻名于江浙的"五杭"——张小泉剪刀、孔凤春鹅蛋粉、张允升花线、宓大昌烟丝、王星记扇子都出于此地。许多杭州人买东西就是认准这些老字号，不惜从其他城区老远赶过来。还有大批的外地香客，每年趁进城上香之际，都会来孔凤春香粉店买鹅蛋粉、生发油，到方裕和南北货店带南货北货，到张允升帽庄买顶帽子，到胡庆余堂买点膏丹参药，到方回春堂买点六神丸等等。据说大文豪鲁迅就是万隆火腿店的常客，巾帼英雄秋瑾也经常来孔凤春香粉店买香粉带回绍兴。此外，河坊街上还有不少传统小吃，如定胜糕、葱包桧、臭豆腐、酥饼、龙须糖等。河坊街一带除了商铺买卖，还有说书拔牙看痔疮、耍猴练功拔火罐的，市井味道异常浓厚。

河坊街上最具影响力、最有特色的景点有胡庆余堂、凤凰寺、鼓楼、南宋御街等。

胡庆余堂

胡庆余堂是位于杭州大井巷的一处商业古建筑，作为晚清时期的药局，曾经号称"江南药王"，与北京同仁堂齐名，坊间道"北有同仁堂，南有庆余堂"。北京同仁堂的古建筑已全部被拆除重新建造，新建的同仁堂早已没了传统特色，而杭州胡庆余堂仍然原汁原味地保留了下来。

　　"红顶商人"胡雪岩是胡庆余堂的创始人，他生于清朝道光三年（1823年），原籍安徽绩溪。胡雪岩幼时家中贫穷，无力读书，很小就在杭州城里的一家钱庄当学徒。他为人精明能干，依附权贵，在宦海商界里如鱼得水。发迹后，胡雪岩钱庄的分支机构遍布全国各地，同时他还拥有良田万亩，白银2000万两以上，可谓富甲一方。在事业如日中天之时，胡雪岩创办了胡庆余堂国药号。

　　胡雪岩在上城隍山的路边买了八亩地（约5333平方米），建造了一座富有徽派建筑风格特色的药局。整个建筑形制宛如一只仙鹤，栖居于吴山脚下，寓示"健康长寿"。据传，修建胡庆余堂的木料是慈禧太后修建颐和园剩余下来的。

　　按常规，药局的营业厅应该直接与顾客"见面"，而胡庆余堂却不按常理出牌。建筑物四周用青砖砌了高达12米的封火墙，墙脚高2米，靠河坊街一面墙上书有"胡庆余堂国药号"7个大字，每个字占据墙面约20平方米，非常吸人眼球。胡庆余堂的正门在大井巷内，青石库门坐西朝东，门楼上镌刻着金光闪闪的3个楷书大字"庆余堂"，笔力雄健。

　　胡庆余堂采用"前店堂后作坊"的格局，这也是清朝末年中药坊兼门市的典型布局，这种独有的布局非常适合问诊、经营、生产及管理的需要。

进入胡庆余堂的门厅，可以看到一块铮亮的"进内交易"牌子。过了庆余堂的门庭就是一个长廊，长廊的右壁上挂着 38 块丸药牌，每个牌子上写有一剂丸药名，并标明其主治功能。长廊的左侧是一排红漆美人靠，供顾客歇息小坐。长廊的尽头是个四角亭，右转才是坐南朝北的营业大厅。大厅门额上挂着写有"药局"二字的匾额。

跨过青石门槛，整个营业大厅内雕栏玉栋，富丽堂皇。用玻璃做的前天井顶既防雨又透光，厅内两旁为高大的红木柜台，大厅左侧是配方、参茸柜台，右侧是成药柜台。里壁为大型的百眼橱，格斗内存满了各种药材饮片。营业大厅后面原是胡雪岩的账房，中堂上陈设华丽，气氛吉祥，其中的家具全都是红木镶嵌大理石的。现在这里是胡庆余堂中药博物馆的接待厅。

胡庆余堂内还挂有两块匾，是胡雪岩创业时的原物，特别引人瞩目。一块是悬挂在营业大厅内的"真不二价"匾，表示对顾客一视同仁，童叟无欺；另一块是悬挂在后堂的"戒欺"匾，教诲其员工应该遵守制药职业道德，不欺世人。这两块匾体现了胡雪岩"采办务真，修制务精"的办店宗旨。

1988 年 1 月 13 日，胡庆余堂被国务院公布为第三批全国重点文物保护单位。

凤凰寺

凤凰寺位于杭州市中山中路，是一座伊斯兰教教堂，原名真教寺，俗称礼拜堂，因其建筑群看起来恰似一只凤凰，于是在清道光年间（公元 1838 年）改称凤凰寺。历史上曾经把杭州的凤凰寺、扬州的仙鹤寺、泉州的清净寺和广州的怀圣寺并称为我国东南沿海伊斯兰教四大名寺。

凤凰寺历史悠久，始建于唐贞观年间（627—649 年）。唐代时的杭州经济繁荣、文化发达，是我国沿海著名的通商港口，每年有大批的阿拉伯人来此经商。伴随着阿拉伯人的到来，伊斯兰教也随之传入杭州。为了满足大批伊斯兰教教徒进行宗教活动的需要，当时的埃及富商捐资在杭州建立了真教寺。此后真教寺历经磨难，几经兴废。元朝延祐年间（1314—1320 年）阿老丁曾重修凤凰寺，明朝期

间又扩建重修，初步形成了今天凤凰寺的建筑群规模。1646年，清朝政府下令再次重建，重建后的凤凰寺成为当时中国规模最大的清真寺之一。1959年，杭州市政府对凤凰寺进行了全面整修。2009年由杭州市政府拨款，再次对凤凰寺进行了大规模整修，并恢复了寺内长廊、望月楼、礼拜殿、陈列室、水房、殓房等建筑。

与我国传统建筑坐北朝南的建筑格局不同，凤凰寺的主要建筑都是坐西朝东。因为按照伊斯兰教教义的规定，穆斯林行礼拜时必须面向麦加圣地方向。今天的凤凰寺主要建筑物为门厅、礼堂、大殿。大殿建筑是以砖石砌成的"无梁殿"，大殿拱顶上绘有精美的花卉彩图。

杭州凤凰寺的建筑形式继承了西亚早期清真寺的传统风格，同时也融入了我国古代传统建筑的独特韵味，是中国和阿拉伯文化交流的历史见证。2001年6月，凤凰寺被列为"全国重点文物保护单位"。

今天的凤凰寺占地面积约2600平方米，建筑面积约1370平方米，是穆斯林举办宗教节庆活动的主要场所，也是杭州伊斯兰教教徒礼拜的集聚地。

鼓楼

鼓楼是杭州的标志性建筑之一，它的西端连接着吴山。

鼓楼的周边极具市井风情，以前沿街的房子都是两层木结构楼，有许多小店铺、小作坊，诸如小百货店、小点心店、土特产店，还有弹棉花的、做木桶的、做竹椅子的、敲白铁皮的等等。

鼓楼的历史可以追溯到吴越国时期。1100多年前，吴越国国王钱镠把杭州作为吴越国的都城。出于政治、军事和经济上的考虑，钱镠在隋唐杭州城的基础上，曾先后多次改造扩建杭州城。经过钱镠的多次扩建，当时杭城的范围从今天的钱塘江边开始，南起六和塔，东至东河西岸，西到雷峰塔，北达武林门外的夹城巷和艮山门外，形如腰果，所以当时的杭城又称腰果城。钱镠在改造杭城的同时，又在城内修筑了"子城"和"罗城"。"子城"即皇城，"罗城"就是子城以外的外城，而子城和罗城的分界线就是鼓楼。那时候的鼓楼还不叫"鼓楼"，而是叫"朝

天门"。钱镠当初建楼取名"朝天门"，其意是让老百姓尊上、诚服。朝天门楼基高 8 米，东西宽 84 米，南北宽大约 40 米。包括楼基，整个城楼高达 20 米左右。登上鼓楼极目远眺，可远观钱塘江。朝天门就如同一道屏障把皇城和市井两个世界分隔开来。朝天门以南是吴越国皇城及大大小小的衙门，朝天门以北就是黎民百姓的天下。北边商铺林立、人潮涌动，充斥着浓郁的市井气息，与南边的皇城形成鲜明的对比。

"文革"时期鼓楼被拆除，2002 年又重新修复。重建后的鼓楼采用二重檐歇山顶风格，是明代鼓楼建筑的形式。今天的鼓楼高 19.8 米，建筑面积 1046 平方米，底层为文物展示厅，从南面可登上城楼，楼中挂有九面鼓，观景台上悬挂着一口大钟，为"世纪平安钟"。

鼓楼自始建以来，晨钟暮鼓，历尽沧桑，目睹了南宋的山河破碎、明朝的大火焚毁、元朝的拆墙毁城、清朝的日商霸市、"文革"时期的强行拆除等等一系列动荡。直至今日，它依然矗立在那里，默默地傍依着这繁华的市井。

南宋御街

杭州横穿南北的中山路，早在 800 多年前，就是南宋都城临安城中南北走向的主轴线御街，此后也一直是杭州重要的城市商业中心所在地和老城的中轴线。

所谓御街，就是南宋时皇帝出宫行经的道路。南宋皇帝的行宫在凤凰山东麓，他为什么要兴师动众地外出呢？原来是皇帝的家庙景灵宫在城北，就是今天的武林路西侧。景灵宫里供奉着皇帝祖宗的塑像，皇帝每年都要去祭祀四次，祭祀时间是在每个季度的第一个月。另外，凡列祖列宗的逝世周年纪念日，皇帝也要去景灵宫祭祀，并且在次日，皇后及其他皇亲国戚都要前往祭祀一次。如此算来，皇帝皇后及皇亲国戚每年都要多次往返景灵宫，同行的还有众多的文武百官和庞大的仪仗队。为方便皇帝一行的出行，专门修筑了供圣驾行经的御街。御街南起皇城北大门和宁门外，一路向北过朝天门、众安桥、观桥，然后向西沿着贡院路，过新庄桥到达景灵宫。御街全长约 4180 米，据说当时铺设御街路面耗用了三万多块巨石板。由此可见，当初南宋御街的修筑主要是出于政治上的需要。

经过开发整治，今天的南宋御街南北全长 4.3 千米，区块总面积约 87 公顷，已经被打造成宜居、宜商、宜游的特色城市空间，号称中国品质生活第一街。

河坊街上值得回味的历史沉淀很多，老街、古巷、老铺、美食、小吃、名人故居……今天的河坊街不仅是展现杭州历史文化风貌的街道之一，也是西湖申报世界历史文化遗产的有机组成部分。

Qinghefang Historical and Cultural Block

Hefang Street is the only historical street that preserves the ancient city's look. It has been awarded as a AAAA scenic area by National Tourism Administration. Celebrities, ancient alleys, residences, stores add radiance and beauty to the street. It plays an important role in city culture.

Qinghefang Historical and Cultural Block is the most famous one among a dozen of historical blocks in Hangzhou. It is located in the northern foot of Wu Hill which is adjacent to Westlake Scenic Area. It has a full length of 1800 meters and a width of 13 meters from Jiangcheng Road in the east to Nanshan Road in the west. It covers an area of 13.66 hectares. In the Southern Song Dynasty (1127 A.D.–1279 A.D.), Qinghefang Block was outside of the imperial city of Hangzhou, which was next to Emperor Zhaogou's Deshou Palace and Imperial Street. In the Qing Dynasty (1616 A.D.–1911 A.D.), Hefang Street was the power center in which a number of government offices were located. Therefore, many alleys' names had something to do with those offices. In the late Qing Dynasty and early period of the Republic of China (1912 A.D.– 1949 A.D.), numerous shops and stores swarmed in Hefang Street. Snacks, antiques, calligraphy, paintings, time-honored brands flooded the street such as Hu Qingyutang Chinese Pharmacy, Fang Yuhe Shop, Bian Fumao Shoe Store, Shao zhiyan Brush House, and so on. The Four Corners at the crossing of

Hefang Street and Zhongshanzhong Road were occupied by four well-known shops—Kong Fengchun Cosmetics Shop, Fu Dachang Tobacconist, Wan Long Ham Store, Zhang Yunsheng Hat Shop, forming a well-known business center. Five Hangzhou Specialties were quite famous in Yangtze River Delta. They were Zhang Xiaoquan Scissors, Kong Fengchun Oval Powder, Zhang Yunsheng Silver Thread, Fu Dachang Tobacco, and Wang Xingji Fan. The natives traveled a long distance from other districts to make purchase of these time-honored brands. In addition, non-locals who went to temples in Hangzhou to pray would buy stuff from these stores, such as Kong Fengchun's oval powder, hair oil, southern and northern goods from Fang Yuhe Shop, Zhang Yunsheng's hats, Hu Qingyutang Chinese Pharmacy's cream and medicine, as well as Fanghui Chun Tang's Liu Shen Wan (six miraculous herbs pills), to name a few. It is said that Lu Xun, one of China's greatest writers, was a regular customer of Wan Long Ham Store. So was Qiu Jin, a Chinese heroine. She got back home of Shaoxing with powder bought from Kong Fengchun's. Traditional snacks can be seen in Hefang Street here and there, for example, Victory Cake, Shallot Stuffed Pancake, strong-smelling preserved bean curd, flaky pastry, Dragon beard candy and the like. In addition, Hefang Street also witnessed storytelling entertainers, dentists, doctors of haemorrhoids, monkey show players, Tai chi players, cupping therapy practitioners in the market.

The most influential and distinctive scenic spots along Hefang Street include Hu Qingyutang Chinese Pharmacy, Phoenix Mosque, Drum Tower, Southern Song Imperial Street and so on.

Hu Qingyutang Chinese Pharmacy

Hu Qingyutang Chinese Pharmacy is an ancient business building built in late Qing Dynasty, which is located in Dajing Alley as a dispensary. It was called Medicine King in the south of Yangtze River back in old times, which was as famous as Beijing Tongrentang. As a saying goes, in Northern China there is a Tongrentang, while in Southern China Hu Qingyutang. The ancient buildings of Beijing Tongrentang had been demolished and the newly-built one is weak in retaining traditional features. While the features of Hangzhou Hu Qingyutang are still well preserved.

Hu Xueyan, the "red-crown merchant", is the founder of Hu Qingyutang. He was born in 1823 in the city of Jixi, Anhui Province. Without financial support from family, Mr. Hu dropped out of school in early childhood and worked as an apprentice in an old-style private bank in Hangzhou. Being competent and sociable, he made acquaintance with several influential officials and acted like a duck to water in government and business. Gradually, Mr. Hu gained fame and fortune with his private bank branches all over China, fertile farmland of over 10,000 *mu* (about 6.67 square kilometers) and deposits of 20,000,000 silver dollars. He founded the Pharmacy at his prime time.

Hu Xueyan bought a field of 8 *mu* (about 5,333 square meters) on the way to Chenghuang Mountain and built it into a pharmacy with a model of huizhou architectural style. The whole building was like a crane dwelling at the foot of Wushan Mountain, implying the good health and longevity. It is said that the wood resource for Hu Qingyutang was left after the construction of Empress Dowager Cixi's Summer Palace.

In general practice, the business hall of a pharmacy is a place to meet customers. Hu Qingyutang Chinese Pharmacy, however, makes an exception.

Its buildings were surrounded by four 12-meter-high firewalls, each firewall with a 2-meter-high foot. On the wall facing the Hefang Street have 7 Chinese characters meaning "Hu Qingyutang, a time-honored brand". Each character on the wall spans about 20 square meters, which is eye-catching and can be noticed far from distance. The pharmacy's front door is in Dajing Alley. The Stone Gate is sitting west to east. On the arch over the gateway read three glittering Chinese characters of Qingyutang in regular script with the vigor of calligraphic stroke.

Hu Qingyutang Chinese Pharmacy adopts the pattern of business hall in the front and workshop in the back, which is a typical setting pattern for traditional chinese medicine pharmacy in late Qing Dynasty. The pattern is friendly to inquiry, operation, production and management.

Walking into the entrance hall of Hu Qingyutang Chinese Pharmacy, people can clearly see a sign that reads "Transactions Here", which is followed by a hallway. The right wall along the hallway has 38 plates of Chinese medicine pills with names and major functions on. On the left side of the hallway, there is a line of red couches where customers can take a rest. In the end of the hallway is a four-corner pavilion. Turning right there, customers finally arrive in the business hall. The Chinese word of "Pharmacy" is written on the horizontal inscribed board over the hall's gate.

After striding over the bluestone doorsill, customers see a gorgeous business hall with magnificent interior design including carved railings and jade inlays. Sunlight could go through a waterproof glass roof of the courtyard. On both sides stand tall red sandalwood cabinets. There is a counter for formula, herbs, and ginsengs on the left side of the hall and patent medicine on the right side. A large-sized multi-cubicle cabinet is set in the inner wall with a number of pills and medical materials stored in cabinet's drawers. In the back of the

business hall was the office of Hu Xueyan's accountant. The parlour is of eye-popping splendors with red sandalwood furniture with carved marbles. At present it is the reception hall of Hu Qingyutang Chinese Traditional Medicine Museum.

There are another two eye-catching time-honored inscribed boards in the hall which can be traced back to Hu Xueyan's start-up period. One is "True Quality with No Compromising Price" on the business hall, which means that the Pharmacy is honest with customers from all walks of life. The other, "No Cheating", having on the rear central room, disciplines its employees to observe professional ethics and avoid cheating. These two boards reflect Hu Xueyan's business motto of "Pursuit of Honesty and High Standards".

On January 1st, 1988, Hu Qingyutang was awarded as one of the third batch of Key National Historical and Cultural Sites by the State Council.

Phoenix Mosque

Phoenix Mosque, located in Zhongshanzhong Road, is an Islamic mosque, formerly known as Zhenjiao mosque and commonly known as church. It gained its current name in 1838 with its phoenix-like exterior look. Historic records show that the four most famous mosques in southeastern China were Phoenix Mosque in Hangzhou, Crane Mosque in Yangzhou, Qingjing Mosque in Quanzhou and Huaisheng Mosque in Guangzhou.

Phoenix Mosque enjoys a long history. It was under construction from 627-649 in the Tang Dynasty, when Hangzhou was at its heyday as an important trading port with prosperous economy and rich culture. Every year, a number of Arabs came to Hangzhou to conduct business. Islam was hence introduced to China. Satisfied with the religious needs of Moslems, rich Egyptian businessmen

contribute sums to built the Zhenjiao Mosque. Over the years, It witnessed a lot of ups and downs. During 1314–1320 in the Yuan Dynasty, Ala al-Din, an imam from the western regions, rebuilt Phoenix Mosque, which was expanded in the Ming Dynasty into today's architectural complex. In 1646, the Qing Government ordered another reestablishment, making it one of the largest mosques in China. Hangzhou government renovated Phoenix Mosque in 1959 and 2009. The Hallway, Moon-watching Tower, Worship Hall, Exhibition Room, Water Room and Mortuary have been restored.

Different from the traditional architectural pattern of sitting north to south, the main buildings of Phoenix Mosque face eastward because according to Islam doctrines, Muslims should face the holy site of Mecca. Today Phoenix Mosque's main buildings include the Entrance Hall, Auditorium and Audience hall. The Audience Hall is a beamless one. Colored drawings of flowers and plants are painted on the vault of Audience Hall.

The architectural style of Hangzhou's Phoenix Mosque integrates the traditional pattern of mosques in western Asia in early days with traditional Chinese style. It is the testimony of historical cultural exchange between China and Arab countries. In June of 2001, the Mosque was awarded as the "National Key Cultural Relics Protection Unit".

Today the Phoenix Mosque covers an area of 2,600 square meters with a floor area of 1,370 square meters. It is the major site for Islam religious activities and a gathering place for Muslims in Hangzhou.

Drum Tower

Connecting to Wu Hill in the west, Drum Tower is one of Hangzhou's landmarks.

Drum Tower area is a place of hustle and bustle. Houses along the streets were 2-storey wood constructions a long time ago. Workshops, department stores, pastry shops, local specialty stores were here and there. Many craftsmen gathered here to conduct business, fluffing cotton fillers, making wooden barrels and bamboo chairs, striking galvanized iron sheets for different instruments, and so on.

Drum Tower's history can be traced back to the Wuyue Period in China's history. Over 1,100 years ago, Qian Liu, emperor of Wuyue State set Hangzhou as its capital. Having considered political, military and economic factors, he ordered to have Hangzhou expanded several times on the basis of the former Hangzhou city in the Sui and Tang Dynasties. Thanks to his great efforts, Hangzhou in the Wuyue Period reached the Six Harmonies Pagoda in the south, the Wast bank of Dong River in the east, Leifeng Pagoda in the west, Jiacheng Lane and Genshanmen outside the Wulin Gate in the north. As the shape of a cashew, Hangzhou was then nicknamed as the city of cashew. Qian Liu also built "Zi City" and "Luo City". "Zi City" was the inner city for the imperial family while "Luo city" was the outer city for common people. The Drum Tower was the very dividing line between the two cities. Qian Liu named the Drum Tower "Chaotianmen" at that time with the implication of worship and obedience of his subjects. The base of "Chaotianmen" was 8 meters high, 84 meters wide from east to west and 40 meter wide from south to north. The Tower, together with the base, is about 20 meters high. Ascending the Tower, one could enjoy a good view of the Qiantang River. "Chaotianmen" served as a natural shield between the imperial city and the town. The imperial city and government offices were located in the south of it while the common people lived in its north. The northern part of "Chaotianmen" was filled with lively shops and stores, streams of people busily coming and going, which made it contrastive to the imperial city in the south.

The Drum Tower was torn down during the Cultural Revolution period, and then was renovated in 2002. The new Drum Tower has a double-hipped gable roof which is a typical architectural style in the Ming Dynasty. Today It is 19.8 meters in height and the floorage occupies 1,046 square meters. The first floor is an exhibition hall of cultural relics. Visitors can climb the Tower in the south, on which there are 9 drums. One big bell, which is called "Century Peace Clock", was hanged on the observation platform.

Ever since its establishment, the Drum Tower has been witnessing vicissitudes day and night: the country's disintegration in the Southern Song Dynasty, the tearing down of walls and city in the Yuan Dynasty, the palace's destruction by fire in the Ming Dynasty, the market monopolization of Japanese businessmen in the Qing Dynasty, the forceful demolishment of buildings in the Cultural Revolution period. Today, the Drum Tower still stands tall and upright, witnessing the bustle and hustle of the city silently.

Southern Song Imperial Street

Zhongshan Road, going all the way from the north to the south, was the main imperial street of Lin'an (today's Hangzhou), which was the capital in Southern Song Dynasty over 800 years ago. Even up to now, it remains the business center of Hangzhou and central axis of its old town.

The so-called imperial street was the road for emperor's trip in the

Southern Song Dynasty. At that time, the imperial palace for short stays away from the capital for emperors was in the east of Phoenix Mountain, the southwest of Lin'an. Why would they mobilize so many people to go on a trip all the way up to the north? The reason is that Jinling Palace, the emperor's ancestral temple, was in the north, to the west of Wulin Road today. The emperor would go and worship the statues of his ancestors in the ancestral Palace four times a year, usually in the first month of the four seasons. In addition, the emperor would offer sacrifices on the anniversary of his ancestors' death. Next day the empress and all the members in the imperial family would go and worship again. Therefore, the emperor, empress, other members of the imperial family, government officials and guards of honor would visit Jinling Palace several times every year. To pave an imperial street was quite necessary. People going along the Imperial Street usually started from the Hening Gate in the north, went through Chaotianmen, strode over Zhong'an Bridge and Guan Bridge, walked westward along the Gongyuan Road and crossed Xinzhuang Bridge before they finally reached Jinling Palace. It was 4,180 meters long with over 30,000 giant slab stones for pavement. Southern Song Imperial Street was evidently mainly constructed for political needs.

Today, the newly developed and renovated Southern Song Imperial Street has a full length of 4.3 kilometers and an area of 87 hectares. As an individualized urban space for living, business and tourism, the street is called as No. 1 street of quality life in China.

With old streets, ancient alleys, long-standing shops, delicious foods, yummy snacks, celebrities' houses, Hefang Street, an important part of the Qinghefang Historical and Cultural Block, is a sure destination for tourists. The street today not only features the history and culture of Hangzhou, but also constitutes an important part of the West Lake as a World Historic and Cultural Heritage.

中国丝绸城

　　"千里迢迢来杭州，半为西湖半为绸。"到杭州来旅游的客人，逛完西湖名胜后，几乎都会去中国丝绸城走走看看，在这色彩斑斓的丝绸海洋里，愉快地购买自己心仪的丝绸产品，带回家乡或送礼或自用，不亦乐乎。

　　时尚变化无常，时而绿肥红瘦，时而唐衫胡服，那些富丽奢华、光怪陆离的款式总是像烟云一般，一阵风后就飘逝了。但无论时尚怎么变迁，却总有一种面

料如诗似梦地萦绕在霓裳裙摆当中，以其婉约、灵动的质地制造着灿烂和神秘，这种面料就是丝绸。在众多的丝绸产地中，有一处闻名天下，被称为"丝绸之府"，那就是杭州。"丝绸之府"的名称由来之一在于她的历史悠久。杭州是著名的历史文化名城，有着丰富的文化底蕴，杭州丝绸闻名中外，差不多可以说丝绸织成了杭州乃至浙江省的一部分历史。而杭州丝绸文化的展示之处就是中国丝绸城。

中国丝绸城，位于新华路和凤起路交接处，创办于1987年。这里汇集了几百家丝绸品牌，经营着各种家居服饰、围巾领带及工艺品和床上用品，是全国最大的丝绸交易中心。

漫步在中国丝绸城青石板人行道上，可以看到街道两边林立着几百家店铺，如梦似幻的丝绸产品，色彩缤纷、品种繁多，就如同钱江浪潮般涌入你的眼帘，让你目不暇接、流连忘返。

中国丝绸城入口处有一家从外面看起来非常不起眼的小店，店内陈列着的老竹篮、旧樟木箱等杭州人的老物件，与当下时尚的丝绸制品形成鲜明的对比，给人以浓厚的文化气息和美的享受，这就是"集锦"丝绸店。2016年G20峰会在杭州召开，许多外国游客慕名而来，参观游览丝绸城。趁着这大好的时机，各个店家都忙碌地进行着准备。"集锦"丝绸店的独立设计师张海伦更是忙得不亦乐乎。张海伦一直认为，杭州的丝绸产业只有与中国传统文化相结合才会有生命力，才会被世界所接受。作为中国丝绸城的经营户，虽然守着的只是一个小小的门面，但却负有传播杭州丝绸文化的责任。所以，她的每一件作品都力图体现杭州丝绸的独特风格。

参加G20峰会之余，土耳其总统夫人和两个女儿等一行人来到中国丝绸城。总统夫人由于要出席当晚的宴会，匆匆忙忙买了几件中意的丝巾先行离开了。而总统的两个女儿则兴致勃勃，东逛西看后来到了"集锦"丝绸店。张海伦热情地把她们迎进了店内，随后用流利的英语与她们进行沟通并介绍了杭州的丝绸文化和"集锦"丝绸店的产品。目光独特的总统女儿当场选中了一款印有中国风花卉图案的短袖衫，并问能否把这款短袖按照她的要求加长，然后再邮寄到土耳其驻北京大使馆。张海伦马上表示完全可以满足她的要求。接下来的一周，"集锦"

团队非常用心地完成了订单。在外包装上，张海伦采用最环保且带有中国风印花的纸质简易包装，土耳其总统女儿收到"集锦"的衣服后非常满意，她通过大使馆发来了致谢信，并希望"集锦"能为她保留这件衣服的尺寸，以便日后再来定制。应该说，"集锦"邮寄出去的不仅是一件丝织品，更是一份心意，是杭州特色的丝绸文化元素。

中国丝绸城的每个店铺都有自己的特色，每一个经营者都有自己的追求，有自己独特的经营方式：有人专注于传统工艺的传承，有人勇于改革和创新。

杭州金鹭丝绸有限公司的创始人郭夏敏就被称为传统工艺的继承者。自从1993年他创办金鹭丝绸以来，风风雨雨，艰难曲折，不断设计研发新产品，以"9道精湛工艺，108道工序，32项严格检测"的标准为传统工艺注入现代元素。因此，在中国丝绸城，提起"金鹭"，几乎无人不晓。如今，金鹭丝绸已经有17个专柜，4个门店，更有"绮臣""澜妍色""法澜诗诺"等多个知名品牌。郭夏敏对宋锦这一非物质文化遗产非常重视，保护宋锦的手工艺是他一直坚持的理念，所以他不惜投入大量的人力、物力、财力和精力进行宋锦手工艺的传承和研发。现在，这些工艺制品已经是金鹭丝绸的独家产品了。

杭州四大丝绸品牌之一的"喜得宝"在这里有个专卖店，店长成轻萍是一位平易近人的经营者。1999年喜得宝公司改制，当时39岁的成轻萍承包了这个店面，独立负责经营，这一做就是几十年。丝绸加工工艺种类很多，成轻萍最喜爱的工艺就是手绘。可是，随着人工成本的增加和喷绘技术的问世，选择手绘丝绸的人越来越少了。尽管如此，她仍然投入大量成本，鼓励丝绸手绘的师傅们，希望他们无论如何也要坚持下去，不能让这一传统工艺失传。她经常与周围的人讲："只有坚守，才有传承。"

有人在这里"创新"。"富贵锦"是一个知名品牌，走进"富贵锦"不大的店铺，色彩斑斓的真丝围巾像是许多彩蝶在翩翩起舞，而那些拥挤在店里的女宾客恰似一个个扑蝶人。"富贵锦"的掌门人叫应明剑，他做人低调，满脑子的生意经。丝绸产品很多，但是应明剑只做围巾，极其专注。凡是说到丝巾，丝绸圈里的都知道他。他曾经在丝绸城里创下过几个第一：第一个推出乔其纱围巾；第一个做

"火"了 90 厘米的方巾；第一个把丝巾和披肩混搭成时尚。作为一个原创产品，"富贵锦"深受消费者的青睐，刚刚上市不久就被仿冒，仿冒品材质低档，因而价格低廉，这对应明剑的店铺冲击极大，他发誓要做出自己的品牌。经过多年努力，他注册的"富贵锦"商标，终于在 2010 年获得了"杭州市著名商标"的称号。他在获奖时表示，"富贵锦"是中高档丝巾的代言者，诠释了丝巾的品质和格调，轻奢而不失华。

商家的故事永远说不完，正因为有那么多经营者的努力、坚持、守业、传承、创新，消费者才能够在这里买到"储秀"这样的荷花山水品牌的旗袍、"新洁绣"这样的丝绸居家服饰、"海伦罗兰"的睡衣，以及被称为"国宝"的"万事利"，被纺织媒体评定为"纺织服装行业十大最具流行影响力纺织品牌"的"达利发"，被认定为"中华老字号"的都锦生产品，等等。

今天，中国丝绸城的经营者们为弘扬丝绸文化，按照市场景点化的理念，把中国丝绸城建成了具有丝绸文化底蕴的特色街，通过改建扩建装饰，800 米长的商业街区内，飞檐翘壁、粉墙黛瓦、麻石巷道、宅院相连，极具传统江南民居风情。为更生动地阐释丝绸的制作过程，街旁绿化隔离带上还竖有 6 座精美的铜雕，形象地向人们讲述了采桑、养蚕、摇纺、织造、印染、砑绸等丝绸生产的整个过程。

经过几十年的艰难创业，中国丝绸城迎来了今天传统与现代、文化与经济完美结合的崭新面貌，成了杭州一道亮丽的风景线和杭州文化名城的一个重要窗口。透过这个"窗口"，你会更加了解丝绸，喜欢杭州，热爱中国。

China Silk Town

"People travel from afar to Hangzhou, half for the West Lake, half for the silk." After visiting the West Lake, most tourists choose to indulge themselves in the multicolored world of China Silk Town to buy silk products for themselves or for friends and relatives.

Fashion fleets. The colors of green and red are in fashion at intervals. Chinese Tang costumes and Hufu (a kind of clothing worn by the Hu tribe in ancient China's western and northern areas) have been popular from time to time. Looking back into the history of clothing, luxurious and grotesque styles vary swiftly like a piece of cloud. Nevertheless, whatever styles change, silk as a fabric is never outdated in producing fine dresses with its elegance and flexibility. Hangzhou, a famous historical and cultural city in China, is dubbed as the "Home of Silk" where silk constitutes an important part in the history of Hangzhou and Zhejiang as a whole. China Silk Town is the very showcase of silk culture of Hangzhou.

Built in 1987 and located near the crossroads of Xinhua Road and Fengqi Road, China Silk Town has a collection of several hundreds of silk brands and sells various kinds of silk fabrics, leisure wears, scarves, ties, art works and beddings, making the market the largest of its kind in China.

Strolling along the slate-paved streets in China Silk Town, you are most

likely to be dazzled by the varieties of silk products sold at hundreds of stores on both sides of the streets. Shoppers linger here and forget to go home.

At the entrance to the Silk Town, a small ordinary shop orderly displays the old things of the natives such as bamboo baskets and camphor suitcases. They are in sharp contrast with the fashionable silk products, adding strong cultural atmosphere and artistic beauty to the town. This shop names itself as "Jijin" (a collection of silk and brocades). During the G20 Summit in 2016, many foreigners swarmed in the Silk Town, making all the shops fully occupied with intense preparation. Zhang Hailun, the independent designer of "Jijin" Silk Store, was on the go all day during that time. She strongly holds that only by ushering traditional Chinese culture into silk industry can silk industry be finally vitalized and accepted by the world. Small as the "Jijin" Silk Store is, it shoulders the responsibility of spreading Hangzhou silk culture to the whole world. Therefore, each of its product is unique with strong Hangzhou style.

During G20 Summit, Emine Erdogan, the first lady of Turkey and her two daughters paid a visit to the Silk Town in their spare time. After looking around, the first lady bought some silk scarves and left in haste for the dinner party, while the daughters were still in high spirit. They were attracted by the "Jijin" Silk Store, where they were warmly welcomed by the owner Zhang Hailun. With fluent English, she communicated with them and introduced the silk culture of Hangzhou as well as the products of "Jijin" Silk Store to them. The girls chose a Chinese-style short-sleeved shirt printed with patterns of flowers. One of them asked whether the shop could lengthen the shirt and mail it to the Turkey Embassy in Beijing. Hearing this, Zhang Hailun promised that the requirements could be fully met. In the following week, the "Jijin" team completed the order with great care and packed it with plain and environment-friendly Chinese-style printed paper. Carried away with the shirt, she sent a letter of thanks via the Turkey Embassy, in which expressed her hope that "Jijin ship" keep the size of the shirt for her future customization. What "Jijin" mailed was more of kind friendliness and demonstration of Hangzhou silk culture than mere silk products.

Each shop in the Silk Town has its own characteristic and each dealer conducts business with unique management mode. Some focus on the inheritance of traditional silk arts and crafts, while others take the initiative to seek reformation and innovation.

Guo Xiamin, the founder of Hangzhou Jinlu Silk Co. Ltd., is called as the successor of traditional silk crafts. Ever Jinlu Silk was founded in 1993, since when he has been making painstaking efforts to design and develop new silk products with modern elements. For example, he has originated the standard of "9 exquisite technologies, 108 producing procedures and 32 inspection items" in silk production. Thanks to his efforts, "Jinlu" is known by almost everyone in the Silk Town. So far, Jinlu Silk has 17 counters, 4 stores and has developed a series of well-accepted brands such as "Qichen", "Lanyanse" and "Falan Shinuo". Guo Xiamin attaches great importance to the intangible cultural heritage of Song Brocade. Therefore, he has been sparing no efforts to protect the craftsmanship of Song Brocade by investing massive manpower, material and financial resources, and energy in its inheritance, research, and development. Now, Song Brocade has become an exclusive product of Jinlu Silk.

"Xidebao", one of the top four silk brands in Hangzhou, has a franchise store in the Silk Town. Cheng Qingping, the store manager, is quite easy-going. When Xidebao Company reformed its operation mechanism in 1999, Cheng Qingping, 39 years old, became the franchise holder of the store in the Silk Town and has been responsible for its independent operation for dozens

of years. Among many silk processing techniques, her favorite craftsmanship is hand-painting. However, with the increase of labor costs and the advent of inkjet technology, fewer and fewer people choose hand-painted silk products. Despite this, Cheng still invested large sums in this technology and encouraged workers to insist on carrying on this traditional technology, as she believed that inheritance comes only from insistence.

Still some people choose to inherit traditional silk production technology.

Some other people insist on making innovations. "Fuguijin" is another well-known brand in the Silk Town for its innovations. The shop displays brilliantly colorful silk scarves that look like dancing butterflies. Female consumers flood there like butterfly chasers. Ying Mingjian, the owner of "Fuguijin", is unassertive and sophisticated. Among all the silk products, Ying Mingjian is keen on studying silk and selling scarves and his reputation is widely spread throughout the Silk Town. He has scored many achievements; namely, he is the first to sell georgette scarf, the first to popularize 90-square-centimeter scarf, and the first to make the matching of silk scarves with trendy capes. In the beginning, as "Fuguijin" products are favored by consumers, they are easily counterfeited after being put into the market, which are low-priced and poor in quality. Seeing this, Mr. Ying was determined to create his own brand. Due to his endeavors, the "Fuguijin" trademark became "Hangzhou's Famous Trademark" in 2010. When receiving the award, he said that "Fuguijin" positioned toward medium and high-end silk market, producing luxurious and noble products, which fully annotates the content of silk culture.

Endless stories of the Silk Town are told on and on. Thanks to so many dealers' struggle, persistence, inheritance and innovation, consumers can purchase silk cheongsam of "Chuxiu" brand with patterns of lotus and landscape, silk home dresses of "Xinjiexiu" brand, silk pajamas of "Helen

Roland" brand, silk clothing of "Wensli" which is known as "national treasure", "Dalifa" silk products whose brand has been appraised as "Top 10 Most Popular and Influential Textile Brands in Textile Clothing Industry", "Dujinsheng" silk products that are recognized as "China's Time-honored Brand" and the like.

Today, in order to carry forward silk culture, the Silk Town has been rebuilt and expanded into a scenic area characterized by an 800-meter-long commercial street lined with various shops featuring cornice walls, white walls and black tiles, stone-paved lanes, and interconnected courtyards. Besides, 6 beautiful bronze sculptures are set up on the green belt of the street to demonstrate silk production process from mulberry picking, sericulture, shaking, weaving, printing and dyeing to silk polishing.

Through decades of pioneering work, China Silk Town has taken on a brand-new look with the perfect combination of tradition and modernity, culture and economy. It has become a highlight of Hangzhou as well as an important window of Hangzhou as a famous cultural city. Through this "window", you will know more about silk and fall in love with Hangzhou and China.

东山农贸市场

在中国，农贸市场在居民的生活中起到了非常重要的作用。农贸市场是指用于销售蔬菜、瓜果、水产品、禽蛋、肉类及其制品、粮油及其制品、豆制品、调味品等各类农产品和其他食品的、以零售经营为主的固定场所，在农村的乡镇有临时或定期买卖农副业产品和小手工业产品的市场。

在城市里，农贸市场作为市民"吃、穿、住、行"中"吃"的重要组成部分，起着非常大的作用。农贸市场里活蹦乱跳的鱼、丰富的水果、肥美红润的鲜肉、新鲜的蔬菜，琳琅满目，让人目不暇接。外国友人如果想了解中国老百姓生活最真实的一面，农贸市场无疑是一个合适的场所。

你如果走访过杭州的农贸市场，一定会对杭州乃至中国人的日常生活有更深一步的认识。杭州东山农贸市场就是一个值得一看的具有特色的农贸市场。它于 2003 年投入使用，主要服务周边几个社区约 3 万人以及西湖景区附近的餐馆。东山农贸市场面积约 4000 平方米，经过两次提升改造后，已经完成了从传统农贸市场向现代化农贸市场的转型。市场分为上下两层，一楼经营的商品大类有水产、炒货、水果、熟食、鲜花、糕点，二楼经营的商品大类有蔬菜、肉、禽蛋、豆制品、副食品等，市场总体布局合理，消费者购物便捷。

进入东山农贸市场大门后，首先看到的是市场的水产摊位。这里水产品种繁多、货源充足，除了提供一般性的水产以外，还有两个摊位提供特色品种。"西湖鱼市"和"千岛湖水产"所售鱼类分别产自湖光秀丽的西湖和水质清澈的千岛湖，而且这里售卖的鱼全部是野生的，未投放任何人工饲料，从而保证了水产品的原汁原味。每到收获季节，捕鱼队就会在凌晨去湖上捕鱼，一大清早就会将活蹦乱跳的产品送到菜场，保证水产品的品质。这两家店铺凭着过硬的商品质量和实惠的价格获得了消费者的好口碑。为尝到正宗的野生西湖水产和肥美的千岛湖水产，很多杭州人和知名的餐厅都来这里争相采购。2017 年，杭州的白金五星级宾馆黄龙饭店行政总厨李畅在中外美食交流活动中，为了制作驰名中外的杭帮美食"西湖醋鱼"，特意来这里挑选正宗的西湖鱼，结果拔得头筹，为杭州美食的宣传和推广献了一份力。

说到水产，当然还要提一下这里出售的物美价廉的朱太公鱼丸。朱太公鱼丸在东山农贸市场出售已有十多个年头了，摊主夫妻俩都是杭州临安人，在这里一路打拼，出售的鱼丸已经小有名气了。他们做鱼丸的手艺是祖传的，朱太公鱼丸的原料都是包头鱼的鱼肉，包头鱼要现杀，经剖、剁、剽等多道工序后再用机器搅拌，最后用手工做成型。除为了去鱼腥味加入少许姜汁和极少量食用盐以外，

呈现的全是鱼的本味，可谓是用料讲究，加工细致。这样做出的鱼丸，原汁原味，鲜嫩爽滑，咬上一口，让人回味无穷。2016年，日本静冈县知事神户重敏带领的日本参观团，为制作庆祝中日友好的电视节目到东山农贸市场考察，品尝了朱太公鱼丸，大为赞赏。

东山农贸市场出售家禽采取的是冷鲜禽净膛销售模式。所销售的家禽由政府指定的家禽屠宰场进行宰杀，而这些定点屠宰场必须带有动物检疫合格证明或杭州市动物及动物产品分销信息凭证，还要有两个标识——检疫合格标识、生产企业的检验信息标识，由此来保证家禽的食用安全。宰杀后的家禽，由冷藏车辆运送至市场，从宰杀完成到上柜销售，全程冷链，保证家禽的新鲜美味和清洁卫生。

东山农贸市场在每个摊位上面都架设了电子屏幕，它是市场信息化建设的一部分，是经营户信息公示系统和自制食品的"阳光厨房"。经营户信息公示系统上展示了经营户的各种基本信息，包括摊主姓名、照片、经营许可证、信用等级等，还展示了摊位上所售商品的追溯信息和价格，从而可以让消费者更加清晰、直观地了解各种购物的信息。

针对某些消费者对农贸市场内自制食品的制作过程、原料来源等的疑惑，东山农贸市场打造了"阳光厨房"。每个自制食品摊位前都挂有"自制食品公示表"，内容包括摊主姓名、自制食品名称、食品中是否有添加剂、监督电话、食材的成分等。同时，市场在自制食品操作间安装监控，让经营户的一举一动变成"现场直播"展示在消费者的视线中。这既可以对经营户起到更好的监督作用，也可以让消费者更加了解自制食品的加工过程，能放心地选购自己喜欢的食品。

　　俗话说"民以食为天，食以安为先"，人人都要吃饭，家家都要买菜，要吃饭要买菜就离不开农贸市场。如何让大家都愿意走进农贸市场，都能买到放心菜？东山农贸市场给出了正确答案。根据市场发展的需求和消费者的呼声，东山农贸市场创建了全省一流、全国领先的食品安全检测室。

　　食品安全检测室也是整个东山农贸市场最忙碌的部门之一。检测室面积约为20平方米，配备4名工作人员，主要负责市场的经营商品管理、商品安全检测、经营户信用管理、电子台账录入等工作。食品安全检测室引进目前国内最为先进

的全自动检测仪，可同时检测 20 个项目、50 个批次的抽检样品。检测室的基本条件、管理要求、检测要求、检测程序等方面都按照国家有关部门的规定落实，检测对象、检测目的、检测内容、检测流程都对经营户和消费者直接公布，检测过程全程透明，检测结果明细及时公布并在市场各个显示屏中循环播放。

食品安全检测室还提供名为"你点我检"的服务，就是如果消费者对购买的食品不放心，无论是在本市场购买的，还是在其他地方购买的，都可以来市场的食品安全检测室进行免费检测，食品安全检测室会及时告知消费者检测结果。

东山农贸市场食品安全检测室是杭州市目前农贸市场中最大的检测室，如果被检测食品检测出了问题，除了把产品信息告诉经营户，并要求经营户通知其供货商外，还要把产品扣留下来或者销毁掉，并记录在案，再上报有关管理部门。食品安全检测室的工作人员每天还要检查货源的进货渠道，比如豆制品类、猪肉等，就要求提供生产厂家的发票和出货单。

东山农贸市场还建立了市场档案室，推行"一户两档"的制度。其中包括了经营户和供应商的信息、商品来源追溯和销售去向的凭证等资料，所有资料保存至少两年。东山农贸市场建立了信用等级分类制度，对农贸市场进行动态管理。根据信用等级分类及日常考核，对违规商家采取一些惩戒措施。如果多次违规，甚至不合格，就有可能暂时中止其经营活动，甚至逐出市场。

东山农贸市场作为行业中的标杆单位，致力于保障和改善民生，得到社会各界的肯定，获得了"国家级绿色市场""全国价格监测定点单位""省放心市场示范单位"等荣誉称号。

Dongshan Agricultural Market of the Trade

Farmers' markets play a significant part in Chinese daily life. A farmers' market is a fixed retailing place for various agricultural products and food like vegetables, fruits, aquatic products, poultry and eggs, meat (products), cereal and oil (products), bean products, land, condiments. In rural villages and towns, there are also temporary or regular markets for the trade of agricultural and sideline products as well as handicraft articles.

Food, clothing, shelter and transportation are the basic necessities of city residents, whose diet is deeply associated with farmers' markets. The frisky fish, various fruits, plump meat and fresh vegetables all keep your eyes well occupied. Farmers' markets are absolutely the right places to go if friends from foreign countries would like to embrace the real life of the common people in China.

A wander around the farmer's markets in Hangzhou, among which Dongshan Agricultural Market of the Trade market is a typically distinctive one and well worth a visit, will undoubtedly equip you with a further understanding of the daily life of not only the locals in Hangzhou, but also all the Chinese people. Hangzhou Dongshan Agricultural Market of the Trade was put into use in 2003, meeting the demands of several communities nearby with a population of about 30000 and also the restaurants around the West Lake scenic area.

The 4,000-square-meter market has been rebuilt twice, accomplishing the transition from a traditional farmers' market to a modernized one. The market is a two-storey building with a consumer-friendly layout. On the first floor, aquatic products, roasted snacks, fruits, cooked food, flowers and pastries are offered, while tenants on the second floor provide consumers with vegetables, meat, poultry and eggs, bean products and subsidiary food.

Right inside the gate of the market are the aquatic product stalls. Apart from the diverse and abundant regular products, there are two stalls, namely the West Lake Fish Market and the Qiandao Lake Aquatic Product, where you can find special offers. All the fish sold in these two stalls are free of artificial diets, thus ensuring the authentic flavors. During the harvest season, when fishers start their halieutic work in the small hours, the aquatic products will be sent to the market soon after being caught to guarantee the quality. The extraordinary product quality and keen price have gained the two stalls high praise among the consumers. Many Hangzhou locals and renowned restaurants snap their products for taking a bite of the most authentic West Lake and Qiandao Lake delicacies. In an eastern and western gourmet exchange event in 2017, Li Chang, Executive Chef of the platinum five-star The Dragon hotel, came and picked a West Lake fish for the far-famed Hangzhou cuisine "West Lake Vinegar Fish", which later won the first prize, making great contribution to the publicity and promotion of Hangzhou cuisine.

An inevitably mentioned aquatic product here is the Master Zhu's Fish Ball, which is attractive in both price and quality. The stall is owned by a couple from Lin'an, Hangzhou. With more than ten years of hard work, they have become minor celebrities as fish ball makers. Adhering to the ancestral making process, only the flesh of aristichthys nobilis, also called bighead, can be used to make the fish ball. Besides, they put special emphasis on fresh making, which requires the flesh to be processed immediately after the fish is killed. After several procedures such as splitting, scaling and boning, the semi-manufactured flesh will be stirred in the machine and then be shaped manually. Through the whole making process, only a little ginger juice and a trace of salt is added to remove the fishy smell and highlight the original taste of the fish. The elaborately chosen material and the exquisite process help to keep the natural flavor of the fish ball. With just a bite, its tenderness and smoothness will linger on in your mouth. In the year 2016 when Koube Sigetoshi, Governor of Shizuoka, took a Japanese visiting group to Farmers' Market as part of a TV program celebrating the friendship between China and Japan, Master Zhu's fish balls were served and received high praise from the group members.

All the poultry sold in Dongshan Agricultural Market of the Trade is frozen and eviscerated, and is butchered in government-designated slaughter houses. To secure the edible safety of the poultry, these slaughter houses all hold the Animal Quarantine Conformity Certificate, the Animal Products Distribution Information Voucher and at the same time own two marks, namely the conformity inspection mark and the production enterprise's inspection information mark. The slaughtered poultry will be transported to the market by refrigerated trucks. From slaughtering to selling, the whole process is wholly done with cold-chain technics, assuring the freshness, taste and sanitation of the poultry.

Above every single stall in Dongshan Agricultural Market of the Trade there is an electronic screen, which is a part of the market's information construction, functioning as a notice system for the tenant's information and the "Undisguised Kitchen" of homemade food. The notice system not only displays the overall information of the tenant like name, personal photo, business certificate, credit rating and so on, but also shows the traceability information and price of the

products, so that the consumers would obtain a clearer and more intuitive understanding of their buying information.

Drawing lessons from the catering industry, Dongshan Agricultural Market of the Trade introduces the idea of "the Undisguised Kitchen", aiming at reassuring certain consumers' doubts on the making process and raw material resources of the homemade food in the market. A "Homemade Food Notice" is hung in front of every stall with information about the name of the stallholder, the title of the homemade food, whether additives are used, supervision hotline and detailed components of the materials. Meanwhile, the operating rooms of homemade food are all equipped with monitors, which make the whole making process on live broadcast to the consumers. It is not just a strong supervision for the stallholders, but more importantly, a way for the consumers to be aware of the course of food production and ease their concern when shopping.

As the saying goes, "Food is the paramount necessity of people, while to food safety is the top priority." Eating and grocery shopping are indispensable things for every individual and family. These two things can not be separated from a farmers' market. But how to make people be willing to go shopping in the farmers' market and make sure they can get pollutant-free products? Dongshan Agricultural Market of the Trade has offered a proper answer to these questions. To meet the demand of the market development as well as to respond to the needs of the consumers, the market has set up an inspection room for food safety, first-rate in Zhejiang Province and occupying a leading position in China.

The 20-square-meter inspection room, as the busiest department of the market, is manned by 4 staff in charge of commodity management, safety inspection, credit management and electronic account input and so on. The latest automatic detector is brought in and is capable of inspecting 20 items and 50 batches of samples simultaneously. Aspects like basic conditions, management requirements, inspection requirements and inspection procedures all abide by the regulations of related state departments. The whole inspection process is open to the public, with inspection objects, purposes, contents and process all announced to both tenants and consumers. The screens in the market will also display the detailed inspection results in time.

Moreover, the inspection room provides consumers with "Whatever Inspection" service. That is to say, you can enjoy a free inspection for the food no matter whether you bought it in Dongshan Agricultural Market of the Trade or somewhere else, and you will be told the result as soon as the inspection is finished.

The food safety inspection room in Dongshan Agricultural Market of the Trade is currently the largest inspection section in Hangzhou farmers' markets If something is wrong with the sample, the tenant will receive a notice of the corresponding product information and is required to give a feedback to its supplier. As for the defective products, they will be detained or even destroyed. Accurate records will also be made as corroborative evidences reported to related administrative departments. What's more, the inspectors will check the inbound channels of freight sources on a daily basis. For instance, the producers of bean products and pork will have to furnish relevant invoices and delivery orders.

There is also an archive office in Dongshan Agricultural Market of the Trade, in which the "Double Archives" system is carried out. The basic information of tenants and suppliers, vouchers of the traceability of goods sources as well as their whereabouts and other data like that are all kept for at least two years. The dynamic management of the market is implemented through the hierarchical classification and routine check-up of credits. Any

tenant who violates the regulations for several times or fails in the credit evaluation would probably be suspended from operating activities, or even ejected from the market.

As the benchmark in the industry, Dongshan Agricultural Market of the Trade has been dedicating to ensuring and improving people's livelihood and has gained affirmation from all walks of life. The market has obtained honorary titles such as "National Green Market", "National Price Monitor Fixed Unit" and "Provincial Demonstration Unit of Assured Market".

古荡农贸市场

一群外国人好奇地拿着手机正在扫描鸡、鸭上捆绑的二维码，通过扫描，进入溯源系统，他们就能查询到饲养地、检疫地等相关信息。这一幕便是德国 CDS 公司米切尔·哈克耐尔博士在刘锦惠博士的陪同下，率领 40 多人来到杭州西湖区的古荡农贸市场进行调研交流的情景。"这是我来古荡农贸市场参观的第十年了，每一年都有新的变化，肉制品、蔬菜种类越来越多，卫生状况一年比一年好。"米切尔·哈克耐尔博士笑着说道。

西湖区古荡农贸市场是杭州城西的一家老牌菜场。早在 1996 年，这家菜场就在古荡落地生根，刚开始只是一些菜贩在街道两边摆摊子，渐渐地人多了，就形成了露天菜场，到现在已发展成具有一定规模的室内农贸市场了。走进古荡农贸市场，地面干净整洁，摊位井然有序，没有难闻的腥味，没有肮脏的积水，整洁的环境和规范的经营让人耳目一新，完全颠覆了传统农贸市场污水满地、气味熏人的景象，取而代之的是摊贩统一着装，菜品明码标价，网络智慧支付，大数据实时呈现。

古荡农贸市场的管理标准是"时时清、门前清、落手清、台面清、空气清"，市场内环境敞亮、洁净、无异味、无杂物、无蛛网，地面干燥、平整。干净、亮堂、整齐、防滑是最基本的要求。

　　古荡农贸市场是一幢有 2100 平方米的三层大楼：半地下的一楼以经营水产和蔬菜为主；二楼以经营蔬果、豆制品、杂粮为主；三楼经营肉类、干货、鸡蛋等。新招牌，新柜台，不少摊主还在摊位里自发添置了展架，把天南地北的农贸产品摆出了多种艺术造型。卖鸡蛋的经营户喜欢朴实的竹篮，再现鸡蛋、鸭蛋、鹅蛋在农场里诞生后的亲切样貌；出售干货的经营户喜欢把色样各异的塑料盒码得整整齐齐；在腌制品摊位上，经营户用不锈钢盘的冷峻衬托咸肉的鲜香；在粮食制品摊位上，则定制了超级米架，一袋袋大米直接上墙，尽收眼底。

　　古荡农贸市场给人的第一印象是鲜艳明丽。亮丽的柜台，配上绿油油的叶菜、紫色的茄子、红彤彤的番茄、金灿灿的玉米棒……足够凑齐一道彩虹。在二楼和三楼大厅的挑空墙面上，设置了 8 个 1 米多高、近 3 米长的灯箱，上面轮番展示着杭州西湖的名胜风景。经营户和进菜场买菜的顾客们都觉得这个布置非常吸人眼球。卖鱼的经营户最喜欢他们透亮的蓝色柜台，"和大海一样，透着鲜活"。蔬菜柜台都是明亮的黄色，格外接地气。三楼的店铺招牌是正气的大红色，配上红色灯罩的 LED 灯，使这里的商品闪闪发亮。

食品安全管理是古荡农贸市场最为重视的一项工作。检测室配置检测设备和检测人员，每天对市场内销售的蔬菜、水果进行农药残留检测，并做好检测记录，或与有资质的质量检验中心签订定期送检协议。设置规范的市场食品准入档案柜，建立食品安全质量档案。建立健全食品质量查验登记制度。古荡农贸市场还每天派专人检查场内经营者的重要食品进货凭证，审核重要食品供应商的经营资质和实际经营情况。同时，建立健全公示制度。在农贸市场入口处等显眼位置设置宣传栏和公示栏，向消费者公示与交易相关的基本事项和重大事项。

古荡农贸市场的食品安全管理由一系列强组合拳来架构，主要包括商品准入把关机制、质量追溯管理机制、定性定量检测机制、日常巡检机制、不合格品撤柜下架和销毁机制、信息公示与上报机制、台账管理机制等。现在市场检测室建有本市最先进的 5 代农药残留和试剂检测设施，日均覆盖 65 种农产品抽样检测。市场每年将 32 万条购货票证信息输入电脑，并加强对供方单位信息凭证管理，坚持每天打卡、打票、刷卡。为保障消费者吃得更加安心，市场于 2004 年率先推行使用可降解生物环保塑料袋，禁止出售猪肉废油脂、淋巴、肌瘤等废肉料，更好地保障了食品安全。

古荡农贸市场在食品安全上提出，要抓好"早知道""马上知道""全知道"三个"知道"理念，以有效破解食品准入和食品安全管理瓶颈。即通过清晨全面检查票证、实物相符性，电子输入溯源，让市场领导、管理员和经营者对商品货源数量等信息"早知道"；通过检测室清晨快速检测和公示检测结果、动态检测视频，让市场管理方、经营方、消费者"马上知道"；通过多套电子屏系统、百多探头监控系统、摊位电子视频信用监管体系，让管理方、消费者、上级部门、社会各界立即"全知道"市场每个摊位、每条通道、每个角落实事情况和经营户信用表现。

除了每天的例行抽检，市场还制定了一系列的食品安全规则。经营户都说在这里做生意，规矩最多，但是他们又都特别愿意在这里经营。市场要求经营户做

生意一定要诚实守信，不能欺行霸市、短斤缺两，而且要保证食品新鲜度。市场里人人都知道，想要在这里做生意，必须得诚实守信。

　　农贸市场无疑是体现市井文化的一个良好场所。古荡农贸市场曾经接待了芬兰总理、厄瓜多尔前总统等几十个国家的代表，得到了客人的好评。美国鹰之翔公司为了拍摄纪录片《膳食长寿》，曾来古荡农贸市场进行拍摄记录，这档节目向全世界 140 个国家播放。

Gudang Farmers' Market

A group of foreigners were curiously scanning the QR (quick response) code on the chicken and ducks with their mobile phones. After entering the tracing system, they immediately got the information of chicken and ducks' breeding site, place of quarantine and other related information. This happened when Dr. Mitchell from the CDS Company (Germany), accompanied by Dr. Liu Jinhui, was leading a group of more than 40 people to investigate at Gudang Farmers' Market in Xihu District of Hangzhou, Zhejiang Province. "This is the 10th year of my visit to Gudang Farmers' Market. Each year, new changes happen. There are more and more meat products and vegetables, and the sanitary condition is better year by year." said Dr. Mitchell with a smile.

Gudang Farmers' Market is an old-brand farmers' market in the west of Hangzhou and was established early in 1996. In the beginning, only a few vendors sold vegetables on the street. Gradually, more and more vendors gathered here and it became an open-air farmers' market. At present, it has been developed into an indoor farmers' market. When entering Gudang Farmers' Market, one would be impressed by the clean ground, well-organized stalls, clean environment and regulated operation without unpleasant smell or

dirty water. It is totally different from traditional farmers' market that is dirty with stinking waste water running on the ground. Instead, it is featured by vendors in uniform dressing, clearly-marked market price of the vegetable, online payment, real-time presentation of big data.

The management motto of Gudang Farmers' Market is to "keep the front area, desk and air clean after operation at all time", keep the environment bright and clean with no bad smell, debris or spider web, and keep the ground dry and smooth. Having clean, bright, tidy, and anti-skidding environment is the most basic requirements.

Gudang Farmers' Market is a three-storey building with a floor area of 2,100 square meters. The semi-underground floor mainly sells aquatic products and vegetables; the second floor mainly sells vegetables, fruits, soy products and miscellaneous grains; the third floor sells meats, dry goods and eggs. New signboards and counters are seen everywhere. Many stall owners spontaneously set up display racks and arrange various farmers' products from north and south in an artistic style. The owners of the egg stalls prefer simple bamboo baskets and arrange the chicken eggs, duck eggs and goose eggs as what they were after being laid in the farm. Vendors selling dry goods prefer to arrange the various plastic boxes of different colors neatly. At the preserved foods booth, the vendors put away delicious bacons against the coldness of stainless plates; the grain product booths on the ground floor customize super rice racks to display bags of rice on the wall.

On entering Gudang Farmers' Market, the first impression is that it is bright and colorful. The brilliant counters, covered with green leaves, purple eggplants, red tomatoes, golden corncobs, are enough to make a rainbow. On the lofty hollowed walls on the second and third floors, there are eight light boxes of 1 meter in height and nearly 3 meters in length, displaying the pictures of the famous scenic spots of the West Lake. Both vendors and customers think the arrangement is very eye-catching. Fish vendors prefer the bright blue counters. "It looks fresh like the sea." All the vegetable counters are in bright yellow and are especially down-to-earth. On the third floor, bright red shop signs well set off the red shades of LED lights, which makes these goods shining.

Food safety management is the most important work in Gudang Farmers' Market. The testing room, equipped with related equipment and personnel, tests the pesticide residues on vegetables and fruits sold in the market every day and makes testing records, or signs regular inspection agreement with qualified inspection centers. There are standard market food access filing cabinets and food safety & quality records. The market has established a sound food quality inspection and registration system, and has assigned special personnel to check the food purchase vouchers of the operators, audit the operation qualification and the actual operation status of key food suppliers. In addition, the market has established a publicity system. Billboards and Notices are set at the prominent position at the entrance to the farmers' market to announce to consumers the basic and major matters related to the transaction of the markets.

The food safety management system of Gudang Farmers' Market is composed of a series of forceful measures, mainly: commodity access control, quality traceability management, qualitative and quantitative inspection, daily inspection mechanism, unqualified product removal and destruction mechanism, information disclosure and reporting mechanism, account management. Now, the market's testing room has built the most advanced G5 pesticide residues and reagent testing facilities in Hangzhou, Zhejiang Province. About 65 varieties of agricultural products receive sample testing

every day. Every year, the market inputs 320,000 entries of purchase ticket information into the computer, strengthens the management of information certification of the supplying units and insists on daily punching of cards & tickets and swiping of cards. For ensuring consumers's dietary safety the market took the lead in China to promote the wide use of biodegradable and bio-friendly plastic bags in 2004 and banned the sales of pork waste oil, lymph, fibroids and other waste meats.

Gudang Farmers' Market puts forward the "three knowings" concept, "knowing early, knowing immediately and knowing all". This concept effectively breaks the bottleneck in food admission and food safety management. Consequently, make market leaders, managers and operators know early of the commodity supply source, quantity and other information through comprehensive inspection of ticket and certificates, the physical conformity, the electronic input traceability. Market managers, operators and consumers know immediately through express test and publication of the test results by the testing room in the morning, and the dynamic testing videos. Managers, consumers, superior department, social circles "fully know" the actual status of each booth, each passage, each corner and the credit performance of the operators through multiple sets of electronic screen systems, more than one hundred probe monitoring systems, electronic video credit and monitoring system for the booths.

In addition to daily routine sampling, the market also develops a series of food safety rules. Operators say doing business in here must follow many rules, but they are happy to operate. The market requires the operators to keep in mind honesty and trustworthiness in doing business and shall not cheat and dominate the market, shall not give short weight and shall guarantee the freshness of foods. Everyone in the market knows that, if you want to do

business here, you have to be honest and trustworthy.

The farmers' market is undoubtedly a good place to reflect the civil culture. So far, Gudang Farmers' Market has received representatives from dozens of countries, including the Prime Minister of Finland and the Former President of Ecuador, and was well-received by the guests. U.S. Freefalcon Company ever shot in Gudang Farmers' Market for the documentary *Meal and Longevity*. The program has been aired in 140 countries worldwide.

杭州市富阳中医骨伤医院

> 2011年7月2日下午1点30分，在杭州滨江区的一住宅小区内，一个2岁女童突然从10楼坠落，正在楼下的吴菊萍奋不顾身地冲过去用双手接住了孩子，女孩稚嫩的生命得救了，但吴菊萍的手臂瞬间被巨大的冲击力撞成粉碎性骨折。她选择到杭州市富阳中医骨伤医院进行医治。两个多月后，吴菊萍伤好出院，张氏骨伤疗法又一次向世人展示了它的神奇。

"治伤如神医，接骨有奇术。"迄今为止，杭州市富阳中医骨伤医院已传承张氏骨伤疗法170多年了。张氏骨伤疗法以创伤骨科见长，以手法整复、杉树皮夹板外固定、中药内服外敷治疗为特色，以其悠久的历史、独特的疗法和满意的疗效而闻名遐迩，声誉卓著。

张氏骨伤疗法在2011年被列入国家非物质文化遗产名录。张氏治疗接骨技术特色疗法主要有：

一、张氏正骨手法。融汇百家手法精粹，创立了独特的张氏正骨术。

二、张氏杉树皮夹板外固定法。利用杉树皮形成了一套完整的选材、储存、制作、修正、塑形等夹板制作流程，在四肢骨干骨折、关节骨折中配合整复手法，作为独特的外固定材料，具有明显的治疗优势。

三、张氏经验方。根据张氏经验方制成的百草膏、太乙针、生肌散、八将散等自制制剂，在治疗骨折筋伤、截瘫和脑外伤后遗症、腰腿疼、骨关节炎等方面疗效显著。

杭州市富阳中医骨伤医院的创始人是张绍富先生，他也是浙江省非物质文化遗产张氏中医骨伤科第四代传人。张绍富出生于富春江畔的上图山村，祖上三代行医，善治跌打损伤等骨折问题。他 14 岁随父学医，专研骨伤科。1954 年，张绍富创办了富阳上图山巡回医疗站；1956 年，医疗站搬迁到东梓关，张绍富在那里创办了东图乡中医联合诊所；后来又发展成为东图医院、杭州市富阳中医骨伤医院。张绍富也一步步从乡村郎中发展成为中医骨伤名医。在东梓关时，坐船来看病的人很多，上岸之后你追我赶去挂号，容易发生意外。为方便病人，他安排医生到码头上发排队号，对那些行动不便的病人，张绍富特意组织医务人员到码头上用担架把病人一个一个抬到医院，场景非常感人，一时被传为佳话。在这样的办院氛围下，加上张氏骨科传人张绍富等医生的精湛医术、高尚医德，短短几年，张氏骨科声名远播，东梓关也成了富阳骨伤的代名词。

张绍富在中医骨伤治疗方面刻苦钻研，勇于探索，成功地改进了正骨方法，总结出 50 余种徒手正骨方法，研制出艾火熏针治疗方法及益肾糖浆等 10 多种内服外用中药，疗效显著。按照中国人的传统，原先系派传承都是在家族内的，张绍富摒弃旧俗，将张氏骨伤技术传于外姓，他一生带出了含张氏子弟在内的徒弟共 36 人，他们遍布江浙地区，共同传承张氏骨伤疗法，真正把"富阳骨伤"弘扬于世。

张玉柱是张氏骨伤第五代传人，在临床实践中勇于开拓，不断创新，通过科研方式论证了张氏传统手法整复、杉树皮夹板外固定治疗肱骨髁上骨折等的科学性和有效性，使张氏中医骨伤医术上了一个新台阶。作为浙江省的名中医，张玉柱十分擅长四肢骨折的整复，对颈椎病、腰腿痛、股骨头坏死、外伤性截瘫、骨关节炎、骨不愈等疑难杂症的诊治有较深的造诣。2015 年 6 月，张玉柱先生成为全国骨伤科"十位名医"之一，这也是国家级非遗张氏骨伤疗法在本行业内获得的最高荣誉。

今天的杭州市富阳中医骨伤医院已经于 2008 年整体搬迁至富阳区凤浦路，院区内建筑面积 7 万平方米，在职员工 500 多人，是一所集医疗、科研、教学于

一体的国家三级甲等中医骨伤医院，也是国家临床重点专科项目建设单位，是浙江省最好的一所骨伤医院之一。

杭州市富阳中医骨伤医院建筑以江南园林风格为特色，用厅堂廊井形式将各个功能区块紧密相连。绿色掩映下，粉墙黛瓦的屋舍矗立其中，从空中俯视如同一个"合"字，彰显了中国人"天人合一"的理念。在现代建筑格局中蕴含了中华文化的精髓。

进入骨伤医院的门诊大厅，首先映入眼帘的便是扁鹊、华佗、李时珍、孙思邈、张仲景等为中华中医中药事业做出杰出贡献的大医们的浮雕。浮雕背面悬挂有用竹简雕刻的唐代孙思邈所著《大医精诚》的原文（"精"是要求医者要有精湛的技术，"诚"是要求医者要有高尚的品德），以此来倡导医者的奉献精神。

医院内还开辟了中药文化廊、百草园、中药植物鲜活标本及中药饮片展示柜。中医文化廊长约100余米，两边各有60余个展板，展示了中医特色疗法、中医养生、中医保健等知识。展柜内陈列有杉树皮小夹板、医院特色制剂、百草膏和

艾条、张绍富先生手书的门诊病历和中药饮片等，中药饮片的展示柜内还配有图片和说明。通过展示，普通百姓可以直观地认识中药，了解并热爱中医中药，以此巩固发扬中医这一中国传统文化。

医院的百草园内栽有150余种草本、木本、藤本植物，既可观赏也可药用，内设的药臼和药碾让人对中草药的加工产生浓厚的兴趣。每味中药边上还配有介绍，扫一下上面的二维码，就可以看到这味中药的药性、历史以及药膳养生等内容，可以说百草园就是一本活的中药教科书。

如果你想了解中医的博大精深，想感受张氏骨伤疗法的神奇魔力，可以到杭州市富阳中医骨伤医院来看一看，走一走。

Hangzhou Fuyang Traditional Chinese Medicine (TCM) Orthopedic Hospital

At 1:30 p.m. on July 2nd, 2011, when Wu Juping was on her way home in a community in Binjiang District, Hangzhou, a 2-year-old girl suddenly fell from the 10th floor. Regardless of her own safety, Wu Juping rushed forward and caught the fallen little girl, saving the young life, but meanwhile her own arms suffered a comminuted fracture due to the huge impact. She chose to go to Hangzhou Fuyang TCM Orthopedic Hospital for treatment.Two months later, Wu Juping was discharged from the hospital. Zhang's Orthopedics Therapy shows to the world its magical therapeutic effect.

"Miraculous treatment healing the wounded; Thaumaturgic osteosynthesis curing the fracture". Zhang's Orthopedics Therapy has so far been inherited in Hangzhou Fuyang TCM Orthopedic Hospital for over 170 years. It experts in curing traumatic fracture, featuring with manual reduction, external fixation with cedar bark (taxus bark) splints and orally taken as well as externally applied Chinese medicine. Its long history, unique treatment and satisfying curative effect all enjoy high reputation in the whole wide world.

Zhang's Orthopedics Therapy was selected into China National Intangible Cultural Heritage List in 2011. Its distinctive treatments are as follows:

1. Zhang's Bone-setting Technique. The unique technique is integrated with the essence of various skills created by other orthopedics treatment branches.

2. Zhang's External Fixation Technique with Cedar Bark (Taxus Bark) Splints. Through the strict material selection, appropriate storage, sophisticated fabrication, exquisite amendment and accurate modeling, the cedar bark (taxus bark) turns into a characteristic material for external fixation, which combined with bone-setting techniques shows outstanding effects in the treatment of diaphysis fracture in extremities.

3. Zhang's Experience Prescription. On the basis of the prescription, self-made preparations like Various Herbs Cream, Taiyi Acupuncture, Flesh Engendering Powder and Eight Exorcists Detox Powder were developed. It effects significantly in the treatment of diseases and injuries such as bone and sinew injuries, paraplegia and sequels of brain trauma, waist or legs ache, and osteoarthritis.

Hangzhou Fuyang TCM Orthopedic Hospital was established by Mr. Zhang Shaofu, the fourth generation of Zhang's Orthopedics, one of the provincial intangible cultural heritages of Zhejiang. He was born in a small village called Shangtu Mountain Village near the Fuchun River. Since the time of his great-grandfather, his family had started their career in medicine, skilled in healing different kinds of traumatic injuries and fractures. At the age of 14, he began to learn medicine from his father and specialized in orthopedics. In 1954, Mr. Zhang Shaofu set up Fuyang Shangtu Mountain Itinerant Medical Station, which in 1956 moved to Dongzi Pass, where the Dongtu Village Traditional Chinese Medicine Polyclinic was established. Later, the clinic developed into Dongtu Hospital and Fuyang TCM Orthopedic Hospital respectively. Zhang Shaofu himself also accomplished the transition from a nameless herbalist to

the renowned expert in TCM orthopedics. When he was in Dongzi Pass, the number of people who came by ship and asked for his medical advice was so large that accidents were very likely to happen when patients were rushing to make appointment with him. To offer convenience to the patients, Zhang Shaofu asked the doctors to wait in the wharf and hand registration cards out. As for those with mobility difficulties, they would be sent to the hospital by medical staff with stretchers one by one. The touching story was widespread at that time. Adhering to such a concept, Zhang Shaofu and his fellow colleagues built the reputation for Zhang's Orthopedics within just a few years. Dongzi Pass has also become a symbol of Fuyang orthopedics.

Zhang Shaofu has always been studying assiduously and exploring dauntlessly in the field of TCM orthopedics. He improved the existing bone-setting manipulations successfully and came up with over 50 manual bone-setting techniques. Additionally, he developed more than 10 extraordinarily effective Chinese medicines and methods, either orally taken or externally applied, such as smoked acupuncture needle with moxa leaves and kidney tonifying syrup. Regardless of the old tradition, Zhang Shaofu didn't keep his medical skill as a secret in his own family, but shared it to the alien clans. Including his own clan members, he cultivated 36 apprentices in total, who devote themselves to healing the wounded with Zhang's Orthopedics, inheriting and promoting it to the world.

Zhang Yuzhu is the fifth generation of Zhang's Orthopedics. His courage to blaze new trails and spirit of innovation contributes to his scientific proof of the scientificalness and effectiveness of Zhang's External Fixation Technique with Cedar Bark (Taxus Bark) Splints in the treatment of supracondylar fracture of humerus, pushing Zhang's Orthopedics to a new level. As a prestigious Chinese physician in Zhejiang, Zhang Yuzhu is extremely good at the reduction of limb fracture and is proficient in the diagnosis and treatment of complicated diseases like cervical spondylosis, waist and legs ache, avascular necrosis of the femoral head (ANFH), traumatic paraplegia, osteoarthritis and unhealed bones. In June 2015, Mr. Zhang Yuzhu was selected as one of the "Top 10 Prestigious Orthopedic Doctors" in China, which is the highest honor Zhang's Orthopedics has won in the industry.

Fuyang TCM Orthopedic Hospital has integrally moved to Fengpu Road, Fuyang District, Hangzhou, covering a building area of 70,000 square meters and owing over 500 serving staff. It is a Grade III TCM orthopedic hospital oriented in medical treatment, scientific research and teaching. It is also a construction unit for National Key Clinical Specialty Projects and the best orthopedic hospital in Zhejiang Province.

The architectures of Fuyang TCM Orthopedic Hospital are built in the same pattern as gardens on the Yangtze Delta, with winding corridors connecting halls performing their own functions. The white walls and black tiles stand amid the landscape plants, looking like the Chinese character " 合 " when seen in a bird's eye view. Such modernized design well demonstrates the Chinese people's emphasis on the "unity of nature and man".

Inside the out-patient hall are the relief sculptures of the great physicians who made outstanding contribution to TCM such as Bian Que, Hua Tuo, Li Shizhen, Sun Simiao and Zhang Zhongjing. Behind the sculptures hangs the original manuscript of the article "Virtue of Great Physician", written by Sun Simiao in Tang Dynasty, to initiate the spirit of dedication. In the article, Sun Simiao elaborated the essential qualities of a great physician, namely exquisite medical skills and noble moral excellence.

In the hospital there are also a TCM Cultural Pawn, a Various Herbs Garden and display cabinets for specimen of herbs and for sliced herbal

medicines. The TCM Cultural Pawn is about 100 meters long, with over 60 panels displaying knowledge about characteristic TCM therapies, TCM health maintenance and TCM health care. Inside the display cabinets are taxus bark splints, self-made preparations of the hospital, Various Herbs Cream, moxa sticks, clinic medical records written by Mr. Zhang Shaofu and sliced herbal medicines. The cabinet displaying sliced herbal medicines owns extra pictures and instructions. Through such a demonstration, common people are able to develop an intuitive awareness of TCM, thus arousing their enthusiasm for it and finally enhancing the people's acceptance of TCM.

There are over 150 kinds of herbage, xylophyta and liana in Various Herbs Garden, for both ornamental and medical uses. The herb mortar and herb roller inside the garden make people appeal to the process of Chinese medical herbs. Beside the herbs are instructions with QR codes by a single scan of which you can know clearly about the property, history and health care uses of the corresponding herb. The Various Herbs Garden is undoubtedly a vivid textbook for Chinese herbs.

For a further understanding of the profoundness of TCM and the magical effects of Zhang's Orthopedics, please do visit Fuyang TCM Orthopedic Hospital.

工业旅游

Industrial Tourism

杭州都锦生实业有限公司

1926 年，一幅产自中国杭州的织锦《宫妃夜游图》在美国费城国际博览会展出。展品的题材源于中国明代大画家唐寅的名画《宫妃夜游图》，画面纤细入微，毫发毕现。观众连连惊呼："这真是东方艺术的美妙珍品。"这幅充满浓郁东方情调的作品就是杭州都锦生丝织厂代表中国参加会展的作品之一，这件独特的中国丝织工艺品征服了来自世界各国的参展商和观众，一举荣获金质奖章，中国丝绸在世界舞台上获得了至高的荣誉。这也是中国民族工业在世界博览会上获得的第一枚金牌。一时间，杭州织锦蜚声中外，誉满世界。

中国的丝绸生产历史源远流长，作为丝绸之府的杭州出产了许多丝绸品种，其中的织锦是丝绸百花苑中的一枝奇葩，杭州的都锦生织锦更是被誉为"神奇的东方艺术之花"。都锦生织锦形成于 1922 年，由中国著名的爱国实业家都锦生先生独创。都锦生织锦可以说是杭州织锦的代表，经历了近百年的发展和创新，形成了以装饰织锦、像景织锦和服用织锦为代表的极富民族特色的丝织工艺，以织工精致、色彩瑰丽而闻名天下。

杭州有几千年的养蚕纺丝历史，至唐宋年间，杭州丝绸已经被称为"天下之冠"，在中国丝织历史上，苏州的宋锦、四川的蜀锦和南京的云锦曾被称为中国"三大名锦"。到了近代，杭州的都锦生先生在"三大名锦"的基础上，对织锦工艺设计和织造技术进行了一系列的改造和创新，使杭州织锦做到了集宋锦的儒雅、蜀锦的古朴、云锦的艳丽豪放于一体。

都锦生织锦的工艺要求非常高，要经过原料准备、纹样设计、意匠轧花、提花织造、检整后处理等环节。织锦产品包括装饰织锦、像景织锦和服用织锦三大类：装饰织锦有床罩、靠垫、台毯、窗帘及各种家纺系列；像景织锦用独特的纬锦组织，或用黑白线，或用彩线，直接通过经纬的交织来表现千姿百态、栩栩如生的人物形象，风景名胜、动物花卉；服用织锦就是用于制作各种服装的面料，其中织锦缎、古香缎等采用特选的原料，并在专用的提花织机上以多种纬色分缎精织

而成。都锦生的服用织锦是迄今为止获得国家金质奖最多的织锦产品。

都锦生的拳头产品还有一种叫"杭罗"。杭罗由纯桑蚕丝以平纹和纱罗组织联合构成，有"横罗""直罗""花罗"三种，而其中以"翼纱薄似空，飞罗轻如云"著称的"花罗"，由于它的生产工艺最为复杂而堪称极品。杭州的杭罗与江苏的云锦、苏缎并称为中国的"东南三宝"。"杭罗织造技艺"作为中国蚕桑丝织技艺中的重要代表性项目，已于 2009 年 9 月 30 日经联合国教科文组织

批准列入"世界非物质文化遗产"名录。

都锦生还首创了西湖绸伞。1932 年，都锦生受到日本太阳伞的启发，考虑

用自己生产的丝绸来制作太阳伞。经过反复试验，他选用了淡竹为伞骨材料，并亲自试制做出了第一把竹骨绸伞。这种伞直径约 80 厘米（2.4 尺），用杭州富阳特有的淡竹制成伞骨，每把绸伞有 36 支伞骨，伞面用 12 种颜色绘出西湖景观。它张开是一把伞，收拢又是一件竹制工艺品。这种伞上市后非常受欢迎，因为伞面采用的是都锦生丝织厂的丝绸，并且饰有西湖风景图案，所以被称为"西湖绸伞"。

都锦生出生于杭州西湖边的龙井茶产地——茅家埠，于 1919 年毕业于浙江理工大学的前身——浙江（省立）甲种工业学校机织科，毕业后留校任艺徒班教师，主要教授织造。1921 年，在教学实践中，都锦生经反复钻研，专心描摹，绘制成一幅意匠图（意匠图就是把设计原图用打格子的方法在纸上放大，再一笔一笔在格子里临摹，同时要确定每个部位用什么颜色的组织材料，这样织出来的色彩才能酷似原画），并在学校实验工场亲自轧制花版，亲手织出第一幅丝织风景画——《九溪十八涧》。这在当时就引起不小的轰动。

在都锦生 23 岁那年，他走下三尺讲台，登上一个更加广阔的舞台。在亲朋好友的支持下，他借了一笔资金，购置一台手拉机，雇工人一名，开始创业。1922 年 5 月 15 日，他在茅家埠都宅里创办了以自己名字命名的都锦生丝织厂。由于都锦生织造的丝织风景画新颖别致，价格不高，很受大众欢迎，很

快被抢购一空。他也自此跨出了"丝织救国"的第一步。到了1926年，都锦生已拥有手拉机近百台，轧花机五台，能工巧匠八人，职工约一百三四十人，作坊规模进一步扩大。同年，因为都锦生的代表作《宫妃夜游图》在美国费城国际博览会展出并荣获金质奖章，一时都锦生织锦蜚声中外，产品远销南洋和欧美等地。

1927年到1931年是都锦生创业的全盛时期，他为了提高竞争力，改进技术，增加品种，短短几年就成功地研制出丝织台毯、靠垫、五彩锦绣等多个品种。他还在当时杭州最热闹的花市街（今天的邮电路）开设营业所，同时在上海、南京、北京、广州、香港等大城市开设了13个营业所，产品畅销国内外。

1928年至1929年间，都锦生东渡日本考察，后来他又从留学法国的友人处获得一台法国生产的新式全铁电力机，又购得法国制造的棉织油画风景作样品，与工人、技术人员进行解剖分析，研制新产品。此后，都锦生将工厂迁到了杭州艮山门，买地置产，扩大经营，改良品种，拓宽销路。当年的手工小作坊已经变成了一家有规模讲质量的实业公司了。

都锦生是一个讲求实际的实业家，还是个铮铮铁骨的爱国人士。1931年"九一八"事变后，在抗日爱国热潮的推动下，都锦生为了抵制日货，停止购买日产人造丝，改用意大利和法国的人造丝。1937年12月，日寇侵占杭州后，到处找他，要他担任杭州商会会长，目的是利用他的声望，让杭州工商界的人士为日本人效劳。日本人找不到都锦生，便在报纸上刊登委任状授伪职于都锦生，都锦生发现自己的名字遭到如此亵渎，不禁怒火中烧。为了躲避日本侵略者的进一步迫害，他带领全家避居上海，并在上海建造厂房，扩大生产。1941年12月，太平洋战争爆发后，日本帝国主义占领上海租界，都锦生丝织厂被迫倒闭，加上重庆、广州等地的门市部亦先后被日机炸毁，都锦生悲愤交集。1943年5月，一代英才都锦生突发脑出血在上海病逝。

都锦生作为一个为锦而生的人，最终为锦而死。但令人欣慰的是，他的织锦技术却永远地保留了下来，经过八十多年的沧桑变迁，成为我国规模最大的丝织生产基地之一。1992年，都锦生丝织厂被授予"中华老字号"的称号。

周恩来曾经说过："都锦生织锦是国宝，要保留下来，要后继有人。"今天的

杭州都锦生实业有限公司坐落在美丽的西子湖畔，它已经由最初的手工作坊发展成目前国内最大的丝织工艺品生产出口企业。

1997 年 5 月，都锦生织锦博物馆开馆。博物馆的前身为杭州都锦生丝织厂陈列室，该馆是我国第一家专题织锦博物馆，也是杭州织锦技艺非遗宣传展示基地。该馆以《九溪十八涧》和《宫妃夜游图》等近千件藏品、实物和图片，详尽地介绍了当代杭州织锦的代表——都锦生织锦的形成和发展过程。同时，该馆还专门介绍了都锦生先生的生平和以他的名字命名的中华老字号企业——杭州都锦生实业有限公司近百年来的创业发展历史。

Hangzhou Du Jinsheng Industrial Limited Company

Dating back to the year 1926, a piece of brocade titled *Night Tour of Imperial Concubines* was on display in the American Philadelphia International Expo. The brocade was made in Hangzhou, China and its inspiration originated from the cognominal painting by Tang Yin, the painting master in Ming Dynasty. The brocade was so dedicate, demonstrating every single detail of the original painting, that visitors all sighed in amazement, "This is absolutely a fantastic treasure of the oriental art." This fully eastern-style masterpiece was one of the exhibits sent by Du Jinsheng Silk Factory, which completely fascinated exhibitors and visitors from all over the world and won the gold medal, the highest honor for Chinese silk on the world stage and also the first gold medal of the national industry of China in the Philadelphia International Expo. The brocade of Hangzhou was of world fame overnight.

The silk production in China enjoys a long history. As the home of silk, Hangzhou breeds various sorts of silk, among which the brocade is an absolute curiosity. The brocade produced by Hangzhou Du Jinsheng Factory is even honored as "the Essence of Oriental Art". Du Jinsheng Brocade was an original creation of Mr. Du Jinsheng, the famous patriotic industrialist, in 1922. After a continuous development and innovation for almost a century, Du Jinsheng

Brocade has become a typical representative of the brocade industry in Hangzhou, having developed several nationally featured brocades for decorative and clothing uses, or silk weaving techniques for brocades with photographic patterns. It is famous for its exquisite weaving skills and magnificent colors.

The history of sericulture and silk reeling in Hangzhou began thousands of years ago. During the Tang and the Song Dynasties, the silk of Hangzhou was already called "greatest of all time(G.O.A.T.)". In the silk manufacturing history of China, the Song Brocade of Suzhou, the Shu Brocade of Sichuan and the Yun Brocade of Nanjing were once the "Top Three Brocades" in China. When it came to the modern times, Mr. Du Jinsheng made a series of reforms and innovations to the design and techniques of brocades, based on the previous experience of the "Top Three Brocades". His revolutionary attempts made Hangzhou Brocade assemble the unique features of Song Brocade, Shu Brocade and Yun Brocade, namely refinedness, primitive simplicity and gorgeousness respectively.

Du Jinsheng Brocade has extremely high standard in its manufacturing process, including procedures as raw materials preparation, pattern design, drafting and ginning, jacquard weaving and after-sorting check. Its products are mainly of three categories: decorative brocades, photographic patterned brocades and clothing brocades. Decorative brocades are basically used to make household textiles such as bedspreads, back cushions, desk carpets and curtains. The photographic patterned brocades vividly present the lifelike images of characters, sceneries, animals and plants through the direct interweaving of the warp and a special kind of weft, either black-and-white or chromatic. As for clothing brocades, they are widely used as dressmaking fabrics, among which Tapestry Satin and Soochow Brocade are made from special raw materials and each of their satin is separately woven with multiple weft colors. The clothing brocades of Du Jinsheng have won the most gold medals compared with other brocade products.

Another knockout product of Du Jinsheng is "Leno", also called "Hangzhou Leno". The Leno is composed of plain and gauze weaves, whose content is purely silk. There are three kinds of Leno, namely "Lateral Leno" "Vertical Leno" and "Jacquard Leno". The Jacquard Leno, featured with the infinitesimal thickness and weight, is rated a masterwork due to its extremely complicated production process. Together with the Yun Brocade and Su Satin of Jiangsu, Hangzhou Leno is called "Three Treasures of the Southeast China". As a representative item in Chinese silk weaving skills, "Leno Weaving Technique" was declared a "World Intangible Heritage" by UNESCO on September 30th, 2009.

Mr. Du Jinsheng also initiated the West Lake Silk Parasol. In 1932, inspired by the Japanese parasol, Du Jinsheng considered to make parasols with his self-made silk. After countless experiments, he chose henon bamboo to be the material of ribs and later produced the first silk parasol with bamboo ribs. This parasol has a diameter of 80 centimeters, with 36 ribs made from the local henon bamboo of Fuyang District. The cover of it is painted the charming views of the West Lake with 12 colors. It functions as a parasol when it is open, while looks like a bamboo handicraft when folded up. The umbrella has been very popular since it was released because of its silk-made cover with sceneries of the West Lake. This is also the reason why it is called "West Lake Silk Parasol".

Mr. Du Jinsheng was born in a village near the West Lake called Maojiabu, the origin of Longjing Tea. In 1919, he graduated from Class A Technical School of Zhejiang, the predecessor of Zhejiang Sci-Tech University, majoring in Machine Weaving. He continued to work as a teacher in the school after graduation, mainly responsible for the teaching of weaving. In his teaching practice in 1921, Du Jinsheng finished a draft with constant study and

devotional tracing. (Drafting means magnifying the original drawing on paper with defined grids. Then manually copy the original drawing in the grids and decide the corresponding color of the weaving structures. Only under such weaving techniques will the draft be exactly the same as the original drawing.) Later he rolled the weaving plate himself in the experiment workshop and accomplished the first silk landscape painting—*"Nine Creeks and Eighteen Gullies"*, which aroused great public attention at that time.

At the age of 23, Du Jinsheng finished his personal transition from a teacher to a industrialist. With the initial capital borrowed from friends and relatives, he bought a manual weaving machine and hired a worker, officially starting his business career. On May 15th 1922, he established a silk weaving factory named after himself in his own house in Maojiabu. Due to the chic style and reasonable price, his silk landscape paintings were snapped up very soon. From that moment on, he made his first step to "save the nation by silk weaving". When it comes to 1926, Du Jinsheng Factory had continually scaled up with nearly 100 manual weaving machines, 5 cotton gins, 8 veteran craftsmen and around 130 staff. It was also in the same year when its representative work "Night Tour of Imperial Concubines" was sent to Philadelphia International Expo and won the gold medal. The products of Du Jinsheng were then sold to Southeast Asia, Europe and America.

The period of time between 1927 and 1931 was the heyday of Du Jinsheng's entrepreneurship. In order to enhance the core competitiveness, he made great efforts to improve the techniques and add varieties, successfully developing several new silk products such as desk carpets, back cushions and multicolored brocade within just a few years. He not only set up a business office in Huashi Street(currently called Youdian Road), the most flourishing place at that time, but also in metropolises like Shanghai, Nanjing, Beijing,

Guangzhou and Hong Kong, exploiting both domestic and foreign markets.

In 1928 and 1929, Du Jinsheng visited Japan and inspected the local industries. He got the latest French-made iron electronic weaving machine from a friend of his who studied in French and bought cotton weaving landscape oil paintings made in France, which were all carefully analyzed and were used to develop new products. Later on, Du Jinsheng moved his factory to Genshanmen, Hangzhou and expanded the business by purchasing land and properties, updating product varieties and broadening selling lines. The small manual workshop had turned into a large scale quality-oriented industrial company

Du Jinsheng is not only a practical industrialist, but also a determined patriotic personage. After the Mukden Incident in 1931, under the anti-Japanese patriotic upsurge, Du Jinsheng stopped the procurement of Japanese artificial silk as an attempt to boycott Japanese products. Instead, he purchased it from Italy and France. In the December of 1937, Hangzhou was invaded and occupied. In order to take advantage of his reputation and make the people in industrial and commercial circles would work for them, the Japanese searched for him everywhere and nominated him for the President of the Chamber of Commerce of Hangzhou. Such shameless attempts were naturally all in vain, but the Japanese continued to carry a fake commission on the newspaper. Du Jinsheng burst into anger when seeing his name being insulted like this. To get rid of the further persecution, he and his family moved to Shanghai where he built another plant and expanded production. In December of 1941, when the Pacific War broke out, the Japanese imperialists occupied the Shanghai Concession. The Du Jinsheng Silk Weaving Factory in Shanghai was shut down. What's worse, the retail departments in Guangzhou, Chongqing and other cities were destroyed successively due to the Japanese aerial bombing.

The grief and indignation deep in his heart eventually resulted in an unfortunate cerebral hemorrhage, which led to his passing away in May 1943.

As a man born for brocade, Du Jinsheng ultimately died for it, too. Comfortingly, however, his weaving techniques are kept permanently and his enterprise has developed into one of the largest silk weaving producers. In 1992, Du Jinsheng Silk Weaving Factory was granted "China Time-honored Brand" by the Domestic Trade Department.

Mr. Zhou Enlai, China's late premier, once said, "Du Jinsheng Brocade is a national treasure which needs to be kept and inherited." Today Hangzhou Du Jinsheng Industrial Limited Company is located beside the scenic West Lake. It is no longer the manufacturing workshop in the past, but currently the largest production and export enterprise for silk weaving artwares in China.

Du Jinsheng Silk Knitting Museum was open in May 1997. It used to be the showroom of Hangzhou Du Jinsheng Silk Weaving Factory. It is the first museum specially established for brocade and also a publicity and demonstration base for the brocade weaving techniques of Hangzhou to apply for the authentication of intangible cultural heritage. Near 1000 antiques, real objects and pictures are well stored in the museum, demonstrating the origin and development process of Du Jinsheng Brocade, the typical representative of the modern Hangzhou brocade industry, at length, including the renowned *Nine Creeks and Eighteen Gullies* and *Night Tour of Imperial Concubines*. Meanwhile, the museum also shows the life story of Mr. Du Jinsheng and the 100 years' entrepreneurship footprints of the time-honored enterprise named after him— Hangzhou Du Jinsheng Industrial Limited Company.

杭州王星记扇业有限公司

杭城曾流传着这样一个故事：炎炎夏日，一位秀才身着青衫手持折扇出游西湖，湖中日头高照，风荷清艳，突然狂风大作，乌云密布，大雨倾盆。秀才急忙打开扇子遮挡头部和肩膀，待到雨止太阳出，秀才身上仅青衫被雨点打湿了一点，而扇子虽湿透，经太阳一晒又完好如初。这就是"一把扇子半把伞"说法的由来，而这扇子就是王星记扇庄的传统名扇——黑纸描金扇。

据记载，杭州制扇业自南宋始兴起。杭城清河坊东面有条巷子，叫扇子巷，长约一千米，就是当年杭州制扇作坊的聚集地。明清时期，杭州的制扇业进入鼎盛时期，有50多家作坊，5000多名工人。当时名声较大的扇子作坊有舒莲记、张子元、王星记等。到了清末，杭州的扇子与杭州丝绸、龙井茶都成了贡品，被誉为"杭州三绝"。后来，由于电风扇的出现，杭州制扇业受到了冲击，许多制扇能工巧匠纷纷改行。到了1935年，杭州仅存的扇子作坊已寥寥无几，其中以舒莲记营业额最大，而王星记扇庄则竞争力最强。

今天的杭州王星记扇业有限公司就是当年的王星记扇庄，创建于清朝光绪元年（1875年）。和其他扇庄一样，当时的王星记是一个家庭作坊。它的创始人叫王星斋，其祖辈从事制扇业，他耳濡目染，又聪明好学，在继承杭扇传统的基础上，吸收他人的制扇经验，改进制扇工艺，特别是在制作工艺上精益求精，到20岁出头时已成为制扇名匠。王星斋的妻子陈英是当时远近闻名的黑纸扇贴花洒金高

手，夫妻俩相信"精工出细活，料好夺天工"，他们制作的黑纸扇，远销意大利、巴拿马等，并作为杭州的特产进贡朝廷，因此王星记黑纸扇又被称为"贡扇"。

1893年，王星斋在上海城隍庙开了一家季节性小扇子店铺，高质量的扇子赢得了上海市民的认可，当年所产扇子一销而空，王星斋也因此声名鹊起、名声远扬，京津一带顾客纷纷前来订货。1901年，王星斋在北京开设了王星斋扇庄分店，在上海、沈阳等地设立多个销售点。同时，他又将杭州的制扇作坊迁至祖庙巷，并扩大工场作坊，广招工人徒弟。此时，王星斋从一个小小的家庭制扇作坊已俨然成为中型的制扇工厂了。此时的王星记已与杭城著名扇庄张子元、舒莲记并驾齐驱，成为杭城扇业三大名庄。

1909年，王星斋病故，其子王子清继承父业，将王星斋扇庄更名为王星记扇庄。他发扬了其父辈勇于创新的优秀传统，率先以檀香木为材料制作檀香扇，并冠以西湖名胜之名。与此同时，王星记抵御了日本扇子带来的市场冲击，击败了同行业的竞争对手，在市场上占据了主导地位。

1929年，王子清注册了"三星"商标，同时在杭州太平坊开设了规模为四开间门面的王星记扇庄。他还不惜重金大做广告宣传，大胆承揽了相当一部分的批发、门市业务，使王星记扇子深入人心，家喻户晓。王子清还抓住了1929年杭州举办西湖博览会的良机，挑选各类精致名扇，参加博览会艺术馆陈列竞赛，并且荣获金奖，名声大振。同时，他又编印王星记名扇品种价目专册，广为散发。

他还雇用翻译，招待上门参观选购的国外客户。由于他的精心策划，王星记扇子在博览会期间被抢购一空，还接到了国外商户两年的订单，外销自此打开。

到了1936年，王星记扇子已占据了国内大部分市场。20 世纪 50 年代，杭州市人民政府发文成立王星记扇厂，选址在杭州义井巷，同时广招失散的王星记制扇艺人，恢复和扩大生产，并在杭州闹市地段的湖滨路开设了门市部，恢复启用王星记扇庄原使用的"三星"商标，使王星记扇业有了进一步的传承。

此后，王星记扇业人继承传统，推陈出新，又注册"王星记"商标。与此同时，生产规模迅猛提升，年产扇子达到了 1200 多万把，产品品种也增加到 19 大类 2000 多个花色，成为中国唯一一家综合性的扇子生产基地，接待了亚太地区、英国等地的多名专家、学者。

王星记扇子品种繁多，有黑纸扇、檀香扇、白纸扇、象牙扇、女绢扇、戏曲扇、旅行扇等，其中以黑纸扇和檀香扇最为有名，这两个品种被称为"杭州雅扇"。

黑纸扇是杭扇的重要品种，也是王星记最负盛名的传统产品，它集中了历代制扇人的精湛技艺。黑纸扇的质量，一在扇骨，二在扇面。扇骨以青竹、棕竹、湘妃竹、象牙、玳瑁等为材料，工艺或烫花或雕刻或嵌银丝，非常讲究，并且每根扇骨都打磨得光亮可鉴，厚薄、轻重毫发不差。黑纸扇的扇面是用杭州临安于潜的桑皮纸做的，这种纸质地绵韧，经久耐用。扇骨和扇面准备好后，再用绍兴诸暨的高山柿子漆作黏合剂将二者粘合起来，最后采用福建建煤的提炼物和诸暨高山柿子漆混合而成的颜料涂装扇面，所以黑纸扇色泽乌黑透亮，具有雨淋不透、日晒不翘的特点。

黑纸扇的扇面有泥金、泥银、剪贴等多种工艺形式，有山水、人物、花卉、京剧脸谱等各种绘画书法作品。一把扇子前前后后要经过 86 道工序。王星记出

品的一把微雕小楷《唐诗三百首》真金全棕黑纸扇曾经在 1982 年的世博会上引起轰动。

除了黑纸扇，王星记的檀香扇也闻名于世。檀香扇是王星记传人王子清的一种创新，1920 年，王子清以印度檀香木为原料，开发了以杭州西湖风景名胜为题材的檀香扇。王子清对檀香扇制作的要求极其苛刻：檀香木必须是印度的老山檀，树龄要在十年以上，质地要细腻、坚硬，木质中要含有天然的芳香油。王星记檀香扇的扇面和扇骨都是用这种印度老山檀制成的，哪怕保存十几年，扇起来依然清香袭人。

檀香扇的制作工艺非常繁复，需要 88 道工序，其原材料和辅料都来自大自然，绿色环保。檀香扇扇面扇骨用的是天然檀香木，加工中使用的胶是黄鱼胶。黄鱼胶是以黄鱼肚为原料经过浸泡、炖煮而成的黏性非常好的黏合剂，用它糊的扇面不会脱落。扇面的漆用的是绍兴诸暨的高山柿子漆，钉扇骨的钉子是用牛角制成的。檀香扇的扇面勾画则使用独特的"拉花"技艺，用钢丝锯拉出大小不一、形状各异的小孔上千个，组成千变万化、虚实相宜的精美镂空图案。还有"烫花"和"雕刻"技艺。"烫花"就是用火笔在扇面上烫出深浅不一，褐色焦痕的图案，

技术人员往往能巧妙地利用檀香自然木纹，借"纹"勾勒出奇峰异山，云雾缭绕等画面，非常传神。"雕刻"主要是在扇骨柄上镂空雕出人物、山水、花鸟等图案。经过雕刻后的檀香扇，芬芳、婉约的复古气息扑面而来，艺术欣赏价值更是倍增。

折扇自古以来就是儒雅的标志之一，在各种各样的折扇中，除了名人书画扇以外，最贵重的一种，恐怕就要数杭州王星记的檀香扇了。随着人们生活水平的提高以及檀香扇制作原材料的稀缺，檀香扇的功能已由实用性转向工艺欣赏性了，

主要用于馈赠好友、室内装饰等。

有人说，王星记扇艺有双绝，一绝是制扇工艺，另一绝就是扇面书画。王星记的扇面装饰内容非常丰富，手法多样。杭州王星记扇业有限公司的数十名书画艺人，经常一起研究切磋古今书画艺术，艺人们个个手法娴熟，技艺精湛，神话故事、人物形态、名胜古迹、峰峦叠石、曲溪流水、亭台楼阁、奇花异草、飞鸟珍禽都能入画于扇面。从书法角度来说，正、草、隶、篆，一应俱全。王星记的老艺人还曾经在扇面上抄录过《千字文》《金刚经》，还创作了《唐诗万字扇》等。这些艺人把文美、字美、扇美巧妙地融为一体，把王星记扇子的艺术价值推到了极致。

在当前扇子生产日渐下滑的势头下，王星记却独树一帜，销量仍不减当年。其还因为生产过程非常环保、全程用手工而获得了制扇业唯一的"国家非物质文化遗产"称号。

在依托于中华老字号王星记扇业而建立的杭州王星记扇文化创意产业园里，仍然保留了杭扇生产古老而又传统的手工艺工场，还有技艺精湛的工艺美术大师工作室，和承载中国千年扇文化和千余件扇艺臻品的博物馆。杭州王星记扇文化创意产业园集扇艺设计研发、制作生产、商贸旅游、文化交流于一体，被联合国教科文组织称为"工艺与民间艺术之都"。

Hangzhou Wangxingji Fan Limited Company

In the old days, there was a story widely told in Hangzhou. One day in summer, a scholar was walking around the West Lake wearing a green shirt and holding a folding fan. The sun was shining and the lotus was adorable. Suddenly, the wind blew wildly and it rained heavily. The scholar unfolded his fan immediately to cover his head and shoulders. When the rain stopped and the sun came out again, he found that his green shirt was only dampened slightly. Although the fan was wet thoroughly, after being dried under the sun, it was just as new as before. This is what people call "a fan is like half of an umbrella." And that is the traditional fan of Wangxingji — the black and gold paper fan.

It was recorded that the fan industry started in Hangzhou since Southern Song Dynasty. There was a place named Shanzi (fan) Lane, about one kilometer in length on the east of Qinghefang Street. At that time, many craft workshops gathered there to make fans. During Ming and Qing Dynasties, the fan industry in Hangzhou reached its pinnacle with more than 50 workshops and 5000 workmen. Famous workshops included Shulianji, Zhangziyuan, Wangxingji, etc. By the end of Qing Dynasty, fan was listed as one of the "Three Wonders in Hangzhou," serving as precious tributes together with silk and Longjing tea. Later, due to the emergence of electric fans, the traditional fan industry declined. Many fan artisans changed their profession. In 1935, only few fan workshops remained in Hangzhou. Among them, Shulianji had the largest turnover, whereas Wangxingji was the most competitive.

Today, Wangxingji Fan Limited Company is known as Wangxingji Fan Factory. It was established in 1875, the first year of Guangxu's reign in Qing Dynasty. Its founder was named Wang Xingzhai, who came from a family devoted to fan industry. He was very clever and eager to draw experience from others to develop the traditional Hangzhou fans. He refined craftsmanship and became a famous artisan in his early 20s. His wife, Chen Ying, was also a recognized expert in applique. The couple believed that "meticulous artifacts with fine materials can excel the natural scenery." Their fans gained good reputation and were sold in Italy, Panama, etc. The fans were also accepted as a tribute to the royal court. Thereafter, Wangxingji's black paper fan had been called "the tribute fan."

In 1893, Wang Xingzhai opened a seasonal store selling small fans near the Chenghuang (Chinese city god) Temple in Shanghai. The fans were recognized by Shanghai citizens for the high quality and sold out quickly. Wang Xingzhai then became very famous. Customers from Beijing and Tianjin were attracted to the store as well. In 1901, Wang Xingzhai set up a branch store in Beijing and several sub dealers in different cities such as Shanghai and Shenyang. Meanwhile, he relocated the Hangzhou workshop to Zumiao Lane so as to enlarge its production scale. He also recruited a number of workers and apprentices. Till then, it was no longer a small family workshop, but a medium-sized fan factory. Wangxingji had become one of the top three fan brands in Hangzhou, together with Zhangziyuan and Shulianji.

In 1909, Wang Xingzhai died of illness. His son, Wang Ziqing, took over the industry and changed the name from Wangxingzhai to Wangxingji. He

carried forward the innovative tradition of his family and pioneered in using sandalwood to make fans. The fans were named after famous West Lake scenes. Meanwhile, confronted with severe market environment brought by the Japanese fans, Wangxingji strived to defeat its competitors and took up the dominant position in the fan market.

In 1929, Wang Ziqing registered the trademark of "Tree Stars" and opened a Wangxingji fan store with a grand facade in Taipingfang, Hangzhou. He spent a lot of money advertising it and undertook a large amount of wholesale and retail service. For a moment, Wangxingji became a brand known by every household. Taking advantage of the 1929 West Lake Expo, Wang Ziqing selected delicate fans to compete in the exhibition and finally won the gold medal. Wangxingji's reputation rose rapidly. Additionally, he published product catalogues and hired interpreters to receive international guests to place orders. Thanks to his elaborate plans, Wangxingji's fans not only enjoyed good sales during the expo, but also received a two-year sales contract from overseas, and its exportation thence began.

Till 1936, Wangxingji had taken up the majority of Chinese market share. In the 1950s, the People's Government issued a document and formally set up Wangxingji Fan Factory on Yijing Lane, Hangzhou. The factory sought for fan artisans extensively to expand its production. It also set up a retail department on Hubin Road in central Hangzhou. The trademark of "Three Stars" was put into use again to reinforce Wangxingji's legacy.

Since then, Wangxingji brought forth the new through the old, and formally registered the trademark of "Wangxingji." The production scale developed day by day to 12 million a year. The factory produced more than 2000 fan patterns in 19 types and became the only comprehensive fan manufacturer in China, receiving many experts and scholars from Asia Pacific area, Britain and other areas.

Wangxingji fans vary in types and styles, such as black paper, sandalwood, white paper, ivory, silk, opera, travel fans, etc. The most famous types are black paper and sandalwood fans, also honored as "Hangzhou Elegancy."

The black paper fan plays an important role in Hangzhou fan industry. Being the most prestigious product by Wangxingji, the black paper fan integrates superb techniques of different generations. Its good quality features both the sticks and the leaf. The sticks, serving as the skeletal framework of the fan, are usually made of green bamboo, bamboo palm, spotted bamboo, ivory, tortoiseshell, etc., and are usually processed with pyrograph, carving or silver inlay. Each stick is polished to the same extent. The leaf is made of mulberry paper from Yuqian Town in Hangzhou. This kind of mulberry paper is famous for its softness and durability. The sticks and the leaf are then glued with mountain persimmon paint from Zhuji, Shaoxing. Finally, the leaf is tinted with a pigment mixing the coal extracts from Fujian and the mountain persimmon paint from Zhuji. With these materials, the fans are thus ebony and rain-proof.

The fan leaf is also processed in various ways, such as gold tinting, silver tinting, applique, etc. Various kinds of drawing and calligraphy are applied displaying landscapes, figures, flowers and Peking Opera masks. Each fan is processed through 86 procedures. The golden black paper fan ornamented with *Three Hundred Tang Poems*" in regular script was once a sensation in 1982 World's Fair.

Except for the black paper fans, Wangxingji's sandalwood fans are also famed to the world. The sandalwood fan is an innovation by Wang Ziqing, heir of Wangxingji. In 1920, Wang Ziqing used Indian sandalwood and developed sandalwood fans themed by famous scenes of the West Lake. He was very strict in producing sandalwood fans. The sandalwood must be more than ten years of age from India. The texture must be smooth and hard with natural oil

inside. The fans processed using this kind of wood would have a natural and pleasant scent. Both the leaf and the sticks of Wangxingji's sandalwood fans are made of this kind of Indian sandalwood. Therefore, the fans will remain fragrant even after a dozen of years.

Processing a sandalwood fan is a very complicated job including 88 procedures in total. All the raw and supplementary materials are natural and environmental-friendly. The leaf and the sticks are made of natural sandalwood. Fish glue, after soaking and cooking, serves as an excellent adhesive to stick different parts together. The paint on the leaf is the mountain persimmon paint from Zhuji, Shaoxing. The rivet is made of ox horn. The leaf is ornamented with a special "garland" technique. Holes of various sizes are hollowed out using a steel wire. Thousands of different holes form delicate patterns. Pyrograph and carving are two more important techniques. Pyrograph denotes the use of a heated point to create burning marks on the leaf. Technicians ingeniously make the most of natural sandalwood grain to create spectacular scenery. Carving implies hollowing out patterns such as figures, landscapes, flowers and birds on the sticks and guards. After the carving craftsmanship, sandalwood fans, retaining the specific vintage aroma, are expected to see a substantial growth in the artistic value.

Since the ancient times, folding fans have been regarded as a symbol of elegancy. Except for the folding fans owned by celebrities, the most precious kind belongs to Wangxingji's sandalwood fans. With the development of living standards and the shortage of raw materials, the sandalwood fan has become more aesthetic and precious instead of a simple cooling tool. It is a good present between friends and also used in interior decoration.

It is said that Wangxingji fans have two precious features. One is the fan making technique. The other is the drawing and calligraphy on the fan

leaf. Wangxingji fans vary substantially in the leaf decoration. The artisans of Wangxingji Fan Limited Company often discuss and exchange ideas of ancient and modern arts. They are all skillful in drawing myths, figures, pavilions, landscapes, animals, etc., and adept at different calligraphy styles, including regular, cursive, clerical and seal scripts. One of the old experienced artisans from Wangxingji had reproduced *Thousand Character Classic* and *Diamond Sutra* on the fan leaf and created Thousand Character Fan of Tang Dynasty Poetry. The artisans deftly integrate the beauty of calligraphy, literature and fans, elevating the artistic value of Wangxingji fans to a higher standard.

Although the general production of fans nowadays is declining, Wangxingji is still a brand of its own, maintaining its sales excellence. Thanks to the environmental-friendly handmade tradition, the company has also received the only "National Intangible Cultural Heritage" award among fan industries.

In the Wangxingji Fan Culture Creative Town, this time-honored brand still uses its old and traditional craft workshops. There are also artistic studios for the fan making masters and a museum exhibiting thousands of fan art treasures throughout Chinese history. The Creative Town combines research, design, production, commerce, tourism and cultural exchange. It is awarded by UNESCO as the heritage center for "Craftsmanship and Folk Art."

杭州万事利丝绸文化博物馆

2016年G20峰会期间，全世界的目光都聚焦在杭州。在B20峰会的开幕式上，国际货币基金组织总裁克里斯蒂娜·拉加德女士佩戴着一款优雅的蓝绿色长巾，非常引人注目。第二天，拉加德在出席G20峰会的开幕式时，又佩戴了一条图案别致的大方巾。这两款丝巾都是杭州本土企业万事利集团的产品。万事利将传统丝绸演绎成"丝绸生活方式"，这让拉加德女士大为惊叹。她认为，万事利让人"生活在丝绸里"，并表示："未来，我选择万事利丝巾，而不是爱马仕。"

万事利集团有限公司前身是杭州笕桥镇的一家丝绸厂，它创办于1975年，它的创始人就是祖上四代都是蚕农，后来荣获"全国优秀企业家"称号的沈爱琴女士。她怀着"丝绸之府要创出自己的名牌"的雄心，带领万事利人奋发图强，实现了梦想。经过40多年的发展，万事利集团有限公司已经成了一家以丝绸纺织、文化创意为主业，辅以生物科技、资产经营、金融管理等产业的现代企业集团，进入中国民营企业500强。

为了弘扬杭州丝绸产业的传统文化，诠释丝绸文化的博大精深，2013年1月，万事利集团建立了杭州万事利丝绸文化博物馆。它是我国第一座民办的丝绸文化博物馆。

博物馆占地面积超过1700平方米，馆藏近代、当代文物千余件，品类涵盖清代宫廷刺绣服饰、明清民间刺绣服饰、各色服饰刺绣配饰及小件、现代刺绣精品及现代缂丝精品、万事利建厂以来各个时期的珍品。杭州万事利丝绸文化博物馆通过丝绸历史演义、丝绸文化及丝绸艺术的展示，打破了大众对丝绸即面料的原有认知，进而深刻体会到丝绸是历史，是艺术，更是文化。

进入杭州万事利丝绸文化博物馆，首先映入眼帘的是内部结构如同蚕茧一样的 4D 丝绸文化核心演绎厅，这个演绎厅利用展演结合的机动装置、全息影像技术、异型载体投影、气雾系统等，通过八分钟的视频展示了丝绸的起源、传承、万事利企业文化等内容。接着观众依次进入讲述中国丝绸文化发展和海上丝绸之路行程的历史馆、非物质文化遗产展厅、G20 馆、品牌荣誉馆厅和国礼馆等。

在万事利丝绸文化博物馆里参观的过程其实就是探究文化、欣赏珍品、聆听故事、学习技艺的过程。

探究文化　中国的汉字里藏着许多与丝绸有关的要素。譬如"蚕"字，之所以用"天虫"造字，是因为在古人眼里，蚕是一种不死的动物，其生命由卵到蚕，由蚕到蛹，破茧羽化成蝶，轮回往复，在古代先民心中，蚕是通天的圣物。还有"农"字，繁体的农字上面是个"曲"，下面是"辰"。"曲"是劳动人民养蚕时叠起的一块块蚕匾的象形；而"辰"是龙的意思，出土的文物显示，古人雕出的龙形玉器，与蚕的外形十分相似，龙最早的原形可能就是蚕。因此，"农"最早的意思就是种桑养蚕。通过参观还可以发现其实丝绸与货币也有渊源。在历史上，丝绸曾经是最早的货币之一，也是使用时间最长的货币。货币的"币"字，拆分开为"巾"上加一横，就是表示用于赠送给尊贵客人的特殊丝帛。汉武帝开辟丝绸之路后，由于丝绸便于携带，易于保存，所以更多地替代了黄金的货币功能，作为一般等价物被广泛使用。

到了隋唐时期，唐玄宗等皇帝几下诏书使丝绸成为国家的法定货币。

欣赏珍品　在博物馆的整个展厅里最吸引人眼球的是两件华丽的清朝皇帝的

龙袍。一件是乾隆皇帝的，另一件是同治皇帝的。同治皇帝的那件龙袍是件真品，它是由万事利集团辗转从海外花重金购得的。这件皇袍由质地偏硬的生丝织成，看上去十分清凉。乾隆皇帝的龙袍是复制品，其色彩相比同治皇帝那件更明丽一些。可千万不要以为复制龙袍是件容易的事情，当时为了复制这件龙袍，万事利的员工们花了足足三年时间。龙袍上复杂的纹饰，都是一针一线绣出来的。九条活灵活现的五爪大金龙，分布在袍子各处：胸前三条，背面对应三条，两臂各一条，还有一条暗藏在正面的内里。这样的设计，从正面看是五条龙，从背面看也是五条龙，对应了"九五至尊"的说法。

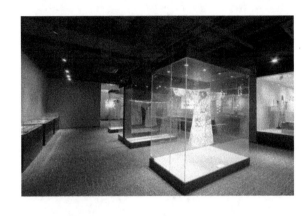

除此以外，龙袍上还有数十种不同的绣纹，每一种纹符，都有特定的寓意。譬如，"斧头"表示一个皇帝必须要有斩钉截铁的个性，"背弓"的纹符则表示皇帝要公正廉明，龙袍上的"海浪"象征着皇帝要像海一样胸怀宽阔，等等。一件龙袍被赋予了这么多的含意，简直是一份皇帝守则，时刻提醒皇帝要自律。

聆听故事 展厅里的展品更让人眼花缭乱。云锦、宋锦、苏绣、杭绣、缂丝、丝毯等等，都是当今丝绸艺术大师们的作品，其中许多大师是非遗项目传承人。苏绣技艺国家级非物质文化遗产代表性传承人李娥英、杭罗手工织造技艺世界级非物质文化遗产的传承人邵官兴、中国刺绣艺术大师和国家级非物质文化遗产项目代表性传承人姚建萍、浙江省非物质文化遗产保护项目传承人陈水琴都榜上有名。他们用灵巧的手，织出或绣出这些看上去轻薄实则十分厚重的艺术品。这些作品背后，还有许多精彩的故事。比如《璇玑图》，看着是一幅图，其实是用不同颜色丝线绣出的字，密密麻麻，共计 841 个字。这幅图背后，还曾经有一个原配斗小三的故事。写这首诗的是古时候一个姓苏的才女。她的丈夫姓窦，去外地做了官。几年之后，有人向苏氏透露，说窦另结了新欢。苏氏便写下《璇玑图》让人捎给了她丈夫。这幅图其实暗藏玄机，顺着读、倒着读、斜着读、绕着圈读、重叠着读，都可以成诗。据说，她丈夫读罢，非常感动，重新回到了她身边。

学习技艺 参观完了博物馆，讲解员还会给大家安排学习系结丝巾的环节，那些拿出来示范用的丝巾，可以说是丝巾中的"LV"：90厘米的方巾，是万事利集团在法国并购的一家企业设计生产的产品，看上去很有国际范儿。同一条丝巾，不同的结法，有着完全不同的风情。

参观万事利丝绸文化博物馆会让你懂得丝绸是面料，更是承载着历史和文化的艺术品。

Hangzhou Wensli Silk Culture Museum

During the 2016 G20 Summit, Hangzhou drew worldwide attention. Christine Lagarde, Managing Director of the International Monetary Fund, wore an elegant blue-green scarf at the G20 Summit opening ceremony. On the following day of the G20 Summit opening ceremony, she was wearing another exclusively-patterned scarf. Both scarves are products of a Hangzhou local company — Zhejiang Wensli Group Co. Ltd. Ms. Lagarde was impressed by the "Silk Lifestyle" and how it was expressed through traditional silk products. She recognized Wensli as enabling people to "Live within Silk." She said, "In the past, I wore Hermès, but in the future, I will choose Wensli."

Wensli Group Co. Ltd, formerly known as Jianqiao Silk Factory, was established in 1975. Its founder, Shen Aiqin, was the fourth generation of her silkworm raiser family, and was later awarded "National Outstanding Entrepreneur". She was ambitious to create a brand of her own in the silk capital of Hangzhou, so she led her team and make great efforts to achieve the dream. After over 40 years of development, Wensli Group has become a modern corporation famous for its silk fabrics, culture innovation, as well as biotechnology, asset and financial management. It is listed among the Top 500 private enterprises in China.

In January, 2013, Wensli Group set up the Silk Culture Museum, which aims to demonstrate and promote traditional culture of Hangzhou silk industry. It was the first private-run silk culture museum in China.

The museum covers an area of over 1,700 square meters. It reserves more than 1,000 relics of modern and contemporary period. Its collection includes royal embroidery clothes of Qing Dynasty, folk embroidery clothes of Ming and Qing Dynasties, colored embroidery accessories, modern embroidery and tapestry products, as well as treasured items since the foundation of Wensli. Through the display of silk history, arts and culture, the museum aims to change the perception that silk simply means a kind of fabric, into a broader idea that silk also means history, arts and culture.

Stepping into Wensli Silk Culture Museum, guests will first find themselves inside a cocoon-shaped 4D silk culture demonstration hall. An eight-minute video, using modern mechanical devices, hologram, heteromorphic projection and fog system, is played here to introduce silk origin, inheritance and Wensli's company culture. Guests will then visit the History Hall that introduces Chinese silk culture and Maritime Silk Road development, followed by halls featuring Intangible Cultural Heritage Exhibition, G20 Exhibition, Brand Honor Exhibition and National Presents Exhibition, etc.

Visiting Wensli Silk Culture Museum is actually an experience of exploring culture, appreciating treasures, listening to stories and learning techniques.

Exploring Culture

Many Chinese characters are associated with silk. For example, the character " 蚕 "(cán=silkworm) is formed by " 天虫 " (the worm from heaven), because ancient people believed that silkworms were immortally repeating their life cycles from eggs, silkworms, chrysalises and butterflies. Silkworms were

considered sacred among ancient people who dreamed to reach heaven and become immortals. Similarly, " 农 " (nóng = farming), in its traditional Chinese character, consists of " 曲 " and " 辰 ". " 曲 " is the pictographic writing of silkworm rearing trays, while " 辰 " means dragon. Historical relics show that the dragon carved on jade articles resembles silkworm. Silkworm is believed to be the prototype of dragon. So originally " 农 " represented planting mulberry trees and rearing silkworms. During the museum visit, it is also not difficult to find out the historical relationship between silk and money. Silk was one of the earliest currencies in history, and one that had been used the longest. The character " 币 " (bì = money) can be divided into " 巾 " and one horizontal stroke above. It indicates the special silk presented to distinguished guests. After Emperor Wu opened up the Silk Road in Han Dynasty, silk was used as a universal equivalent in place of gold because it was easier to carry and preserve. In China's Sui and Tang Dynasties, emperors such as Tang Xuanzong issued several imperial edicts to make silk a legal currency.

Appreciating Treasures

Wandering along the exhibition halls, the most captivating exhibits are two gorgeous imperial robes of Qing Dynasty. One belongs to Emperor Qianlong, and the other one belongs to Emperor Tongzhi. The robe of Emperor Tongzhi is an authentic exhibit. Wensli Group spent a large amount of money to buy it from overseas. The robe is made of raw silk with hard texture and seems very refreshing. The other robe of Emperor Qianlong is a replica. It has a brighter color compared with the one of Emperor Tongzhi. It was not an easy job to replicate an imperial robe. It took Wensli team three whole years for this exact replica. Each complex ornamentation on the robe is embroidered meticulously. Nine vivid golden dragons each with five claws spread over the robe: three

on the front, corresponded by three on the back, one on each sleeve and one hidden inside. With this design, five dragons can be seen from the front and the back alike. It conforms to the saying of the emperor's supreme throne. Besides dragons, tens of different ornament patterns are embroidered on the robe, each conveying a specific meaning. For example, "axe" means the emperor must be resolute and decisive. "Bow" means the emperor must be fair and incorruptible. "Wave" means the emperor must be as broad-minded as the ocean, etc. A robe with these meanings reminds the emperor of self-regulations.

Listening to Stories

The dazzling exhibits, such as Yun brocade, Song brocade, Su embroidery, Hang embroidery, tapestry, silk blanket, etc., are art works of many contemporary silk masters. Many of them are inheritors of Intangible Culture Heritage Programs: Li Eying, the inheritor of Su embroidery; Shao Guanxing, the inheritor of Hang silk weaving; Yao Jianping, Chinese national inheritor and master of embroidery art; Chen Shuiqin, inheritor of intangible culture heritage program of Zhejiang Province, etc. Woven by skillful masters, the silk artworks look thin and light, but are actually very thick and solid. In addition, many interesting stories lie behind these artworks. For example, *Xuanji Tu* (Picture of the Turning Sphere), looks like an ordinary picture, but actually consists of 841 characters in grids woven with colorful silk thread. In fact, the picture hides a story that tells a battle between a wife and a concubine. This poem was written by a smart lady named Su in the old times. Her husband, Dou, was serving for the government in another town. Several years later, Su heard rumors that Dou was having a concubine there. She then wrote *Xuanji Tu* and sent it to her husband. This picture actually contained some secrets. It could be read in different ways such as upwards, downwards or even in a circle, and

the characters could all form poems. It was said that her husband was touched after reading it and came back to her at last.

Learning Techniques

After visiting the exhibitions, the docent will invite guests to learn how to tie a silk scarf. The demonstration kerchieves that are 90 centimetres long and wide, with strong international features and known as LV among scarves, are the designs of a French company incorporated by Wensli. Even on the same scarf, different knots show different tastes. Visiting Wensli Silk Culture Museum will let you understand that silk is not only a kind of fabric, but a treasure of art that expresses history and culture.

天子岭静脉小镇

走进杭州城，映入我们眼帘的是整洁的街道、高耸的商务楼、一幢幢干净有序的居民楼，以及大量衣着靓丽、悠闲自在的行人和外地游客。光鲜美丽的城市背后，几百万人口每天都会产生上万吨各种各样的垃圾，这些城市垃圾又到哪儿去了呢？

城市垃圾就是城市固体废弃物，其中有与人们吃喝有关的厨房有机垃圾及公共场所垃圾、环卫部门道路清扫物、部分建筑垃圾，以及有害物质如干电池、荧光灯管等。由于排出量大，成分复杂多样，且具有污染性、资源性和社会性，所以需要采用无害化、资源化、减量化和社会化的方法进行处理。

处理城市垃圾有许多方法，其中填埋法作为垃圾的最终处置手段一直占有重要位置。将清洁直运车运来的垃圾分选后填埋起来，在上面建起碧草如茵的公园，而渗滤出来的垃圾水，经过重重关卡的科技处理，从浑浊的臭水变成了能直接排放的清水，在杭州天子岭静脉小镇我们就能看到这样的奇迹。

1991年，全国首座符合建设部卫生填埋技术标准的山谷型生活垃圾填埋场——杭州市天子岭第一垃圾填埋场投入使用，2007年埋满封场并实施生态覆绿，2010年建成天子岭静脉小镇并对外开放。

天子岭静脉小镇位于天子岭山的青龙坞山谷内，是我国在封场填埋场上建造的首座公园，公园下方填埋着900多万吨生活垃圾。公园总绿化面积约8万平方米，相当于11个足球场那么大；园内游步道长1400米，建有百果区、桂雨区、

翠竹区和植物模纹景观区，设有摩崖石刻、绿宝寻心、芳园思善、天池映碧等景点，并种植杭州的市树香樟、市花桂花及南方红豆杉、垂丝海棠、紫薇等103种植物。这一万多株植物能够有效吸收二氧化碳，释放氧气。由于垃圾在填埋过程中会产生二氧化碳、甲烷等填埋气体，会对植物的生长产生不利影响，因此，天子岭静脉小镇按照国家相关标准在垃圾堆体上方进行了封场设计。

在这里游览，我们不仅可以俯瞰杭州第二垃圾填埋场井然有序的作业场景，感受环卫工人的艰辛和伟大，还可认识多种绿色植物，体验垃圾山封场覆绿的循环经济。顺着天子岭的盘山路走上半山腰，沿途有翠竹、雪松、无患子、香樟，一片青葱，随处可见海棠、紫薇等盛开的花朵。唯一"露馅"的，只有草坪表面偶见的粗黑沼气收集管，一直通往坡下。昔日垃圾山，今为生态园。

天子岭静脉小镇内最著名的三大景观是绿宝寻心、芳园思善、天池映碧。绿宝寻心指的是绿宝亭，它位于生态公园的正中心。"绿"代表环保、生命与和谐，象征着天子岭人为绿而生，为绿而行；"宝"代表垃圾是放错地方的资源，是资源之宝。芳园思善指的是善小亭，"善小"的意思就是"勿以善小而不为"，告诉我们不要因为好事小而不屑去做，小善积多了就会成为利天下的大善，也寓意着天子岭人以"脚踏垃圾，心怀天下，善小为之，梦想无疆"的胸怀关注垃圾、关注民生，兢兢业业地创造清洁每一日、健康每一天的城市生活。天池映碧位于生态公园东北角，在海拔165米的填埋库区最高处，原为污泥应急堆场。在垃圾填埋场封场后，经清理和安全围护改造为生态水池，并放养鱼苗无数。天池映碧总容积约8万立方米，池内水均为自然雨水汇集而成，可作园区绿化灌溉之用，也可观测防渗、填埋作业新工艺之成效。

公园下方有个市民植树林，内设有"城投雕塑"群，雕塑取"六合相应、和谐共生"之意，代表杭州市的公交、水务、能源、固废、城建、置业六大板块合力推进城市低碳发展，改善生态环境。据测算，树林是最大的"贮碳库"和最好的"吸碳器"，1立方米的木材，能吸收1.83吨二氧化碳，释放1.62吨氧气。每人只要每年栽上3棵树，就可以完全吸收自己在一年的生活中所排放的二氧化

碳，实现"零排放"和绿色生活。

社会各界人士在此种下的桂花和香樟树约有 1000 棵。如今，这里的树木枝叶茂密，四季常绿。金秋佳节，桂花竞相开放，流芳数里。在市民植树林深处，以"废弃物＋创意＝环保＋时尚"为理念，通过奇思妙想，创意改造，天子岭人将司空见惯的废弃物变成生动有趣的艺术装置，让它们重获新生。比如，有尊矗立在城投林上方的"回天大力神"，高 8 米，重 10 吨，取材于天子岭垃圾填埋库区报废的推土机、废零部件、废油桶、废灭火器等。回天大力神的制作完成也正是垃圾变废为宝的一个成功典范。这些零部件经绿色义工、杭州著名装置艺术家周峰先生的精心设计和组装，由其门下弟子与环境集团装备修理分公司多名员工耗时 30 多天装配完成。

在天子岭生态公园还有一个以环保为主题的图书馆。2016 年 6 月 5 日，即第 45 个世界环境日，这座全国首座建在垃圾场上的图书馆正式对外开放。图书馆面积近 1000 平方米，馆藏图书 10 万余册，图书内容包含自然科学、人文历史、生态环保、天文科学、旅行游览等，其中一部分购书经费来源于市民环保众筹。这里能提供专业的环保信息咨询、环保服务预约及丰富的互动体验活动，培养市民的环保意识，并鼓励更多市民参与环保事业。

除此以外，天子岭生态公园还建有垃圾与文化博物馆。垃圾围城，文化解围，垃圾与文化碰撞出的火花照亮着城市出口。馆内作品蕴藏着绿色义工们厚重的社会责任感与勇敢的社会担当。他们以书法、美术、摄影等艺术形式描绘生态蓝图，传播绿色理念，倡导低碳生活。

另有空中花园位于杭州市清洁直运车辆停保场工程顶楼，面积 8000 余平方米，绿化覆盖率超过 90%。花园的设计紧密融合周边山体的地势起伏，绿色环保，崇尚自然，空中俯瞰，宛如天然。站在空中花园高处，可眺望小镇无限自然风光和有序整洁的园区环境。

天子岭生态果园位于空中花园西南侧，建于 2012 年 4 月，占地面积 2 万平方米，园内种植有橘子、枇杷、杨梅、桃、梨、猕猴桃、葡萄等多种果树千余株，集观赏游、科普文化、休闲品尝于一体。游客既可亲手采摘果实体验丰收的乐趣，又可品尝天子岭独有的美食，释放压力、亲近自然，尽情体验轻松愉悦的田园生活。这里也是绿摄行婚纱婚庆摄影基地，是全国首个建造在垃圾山上，集拍摄、观景、游园等于一体的婚纱婚庆摄影基地，拥有近万平方米的拍摄面积，逾百个拍摄景点，如欧陆风情街、天景花园、梦幻空间、鹅池等等。婚庆基地的成立，为准新人们提供了时尚、个性且更具环保意义的全新选择，也为杭州乃至全国的婚庆行业增添了一个新亮点。

"跟着垃圾去旅游"是一条垃圾处理环境教育旅游体验线，曾荣获国际固废协会年度沟通宣传大奖。它将一个又一个处置垃圾环节串联在一起，构成故事性的叙事结构，让亲和感走进每一位参观者的心里。

Tianziling Vein Town

Upon entering Hangzhou, we are greeted by neatly-paved streets, towering office buildings, clean and orderly residential buildings and many well-dressed pedestrians and foreign tourists walking leisurely on the streets. However, behind the beautiful city image, there are thousands tons of various wastes produced by millions of people every day. Then where do these urban wastes go?

Urban garbage is urban solid wastes, which are organic kitchen garbage from people's eating and drinking, wastes from public places, wastes collected by sanitation departments from roads, some construction wastes, and hazardous wastes such as dry batteries and fluorescent tubes. Urban garbage is large in amount with complicated and diversified compositions. Despite its contaminative feature, it can produce nice social benefits once recycled. Therefore, it is necessary to be subjected to harmless, recyclable, reduced and socialized treatment.

There are many ways to treat urban garbage, of which, landfill method has always occupied a large position as the final disposal means of garbage. The garbage collection and transportation vehicles will then transport the wastes sorted out and landfilled. A garden covered with verdant grasses is then built on the ground under which wastes were landfilled. The percolated wastewater is finally subjected to many steps of technological treatments until it turns from turbid smelly water to clean water that can be directly discharged. This miracle happens in Tianziling Vein Town.

In 1991, Hangzhou Tianziling No.1 Waste Landfill, as the first valley-type domestic waste landfill that conforms to the technological standard of the Ministry of Construction for sanitary landfill in China, was put into use. In 2007, it was full, closed and covered with ecological greenery. In 2010, Tianziling Vein Town was completed and opened to the public.

Located in Qinglongwu Valley of Tianziling Mountain, Tianziling Vein Town was the first town built on a landfill in China. More than 9 million tons of domestic garbage was buried below the town. The town covers a total green area of about 80,000 square meters, equivalent to the size of 11 football pitches, and has a walkway with a length of 1,400 meters. The whole park is divided into fruits section, sweet-osmanthus section, green bamboo section, vegetal pattern landscape section, and some scenic spots such as cliff inscriptions, Seeking for Green Treasure at the Center, Reflecting Virtue in Beautiful Garden, and Green Reflection in Heavenly Pool. The town is planted with 103 varieties of plants, such as camphor (Hangzhou's city tree), sweet-osmanthus (Hangzhou's city flower), south yew, filamental flowering crab and crape myrtle. These plants, totaling more than ten thousand, can effectively absorb carbon dioxide and release oxygen. As garbage may produce carbon dioxide, methane and other landfill gases that have adverse effect on the plants during the landfill process, Tianziling Vein Town implemented closure design to the town according to relevant national standards.

When touring in the town, tourists can not only see the orderly operation scene of Hangzhou No.2 Garbage Landfill and feel the hardship and greatness of sanitation workers, but also learn about various green plants and experience

the recycling economy of enclosing the garbage mountain and covering it with green plants. Walking along the winding mountain path of Tianziling all the way up to the hillside, one can see verdant plants, such as bamboo, cedar, soapberry and camphor, and blooming flowers such as Chinese flowering crabapple and crape myrtle everywhere. The only thing that gives the town away is the occasionally-seen dark and black methane collecting pipe leading down the slope on the surface of the lawn. The former garbage mountain is now turned into a Vein Town.

The three most famous scenic spots of Tianziling Vein Town are Seeking for Green Treasure at the Center, Reflecting Virtue in Beautiful Garden, and Green Reflection in Heavenly Pool. Seeking for Green Treasure at the Center refers to the Green Treasure Pavilion that is located at the center of the vein town. "Green" represents environmental protection, life and harmony, indicating that the people of Tianziling aspire for green. "Treasure" indicates that garbage is misplaced resources that can be turned into treasure. Reflecting Virtue in Beautiful Garden refers to the Insignificant Virtue Belittling Pavilion, which is originated from the sentence that "people do not disdain doing anything good though it is insignificant." Insignificant goodness, when being accumulated enough, will be turned into a great virtue. It also implies that the people of Tianziling pay attention to garbage treatment and livelihood, making efforts to create a clean and healthy life for urban citizens every day with assiduity and with the mind of "holding the world in mind while standing on the garbage, cherishing trivial virtue and dreaming without limit." Green Reflection in Heavenly Pool, is located in the northeast of the ecological park at the highest spot of the landfill reservoir area with an elevation of 165 meters. It was formerly the makeshift yard for sludge. After closure of the garbage landfill, it was transformed into the ecological pool after cleaning and safety retaining and has bred numerous fish fries. The total capacity of the heavenly pool is more than 80,000 cubic meters and is filled with natural rain water that can be used for greening and irrigation. It can also be used for observing the efficiency of the new technology for seepage proofing and landfill operation.

Below the Vein Town, there is a citizens' afforestation forest with "urban invested sculpture" group. The sculpture group means "correlated sextile, harmonious coexistence", representing the six sections of Hangzhou, namely, public transportation, water services, energy, solid wastes, urban construction and properties, which work jointly to promote the low-carbon development of the city and improve the ecological environment. As estimated, forest is the largest "carbon pool" and the best "carbon absorber". Every 1 cubic meter of timber reserve can absorb 1.83 tons of carbon dioxide and release 1.62 tons of oxygen. As long as everyone plants 3 trees per year, it is enough to absorb all the carbon dioxide he discharges in one year, thus realizing zero discharge and green life.

Approximate more than 1000 sweet-scented osmanthus trees and camphor trees were planted here by people from all walks of life. Today, the trees here are dense with branches and leaves and evergreen in all seasons. In golden autumn, the sweet-scented osmanthus is in full bloom and the fragrance is strong and wafting far and wide. In the depth of the citizen afforested woods, with the concept of "waste + creativity = environmental protection + fashion", the common wastes are turned into lively and interesting artistic installation and regain a new life through fancy ideas and creative transformation. For example, a work named as "Hercules" standing above the urban-invested woods is 8 meters in height and 10 tons in weight and is made of scrapped bulldozer, wasted components and parts, wasted oil bucket, and wasted fire extinguisher. The work of "Hercules" is also a successful example for turning waste into

treasure. After deliberate design and assembly by Mr. Zhou Feng, a famous installation artist in Hangzhou and a group of green environmental protection voluntary workers, it takes more than 30 days for the disciples of Mr. Zhou and quite a few employees of the Equipment Repairing Branch of Environmental Group to complete the assembly of components and parts.

In Tianziling Vein Town, there is also a themed library of environmental protection. Founded on June 5th, 2016 (the 45th World Environment Day), the first library built on garbage landfill in China was officially open to the public. The library covers an area of about 1,000 square meters and has a collection of more than 100,000 volumes of books, including books of natural science, humanism and history, ecology and environmental protection, astronomical sciences, travel tours, some of which are from citizens' crowdfunding for environmental protection. It can provide professional consultation for environmental protection information, environmental service reservation and diversified interactive experience, cultivate citizens' awareness of environmental protection and encourage more citizens to participate in the undertaking of environmental protection.

In addition, Tianziling Vein Town has also built the Garbage and Culture Museum. Rubbish besieges the city, while culture dismantles the siege. The transformation of garbage into culture reflects the city's great efforts to become an ecological one. The works collected in the museum demonstrate the social responsibility and courageous undertakings of green environmental protection volunteers, who depict the ecological blueprints in the form of calligraphy, art, photography and other artistic forms, spreading green concept and advocating low-carbon life.

Besides, the hanging garden is located on the top floor of Hangzhou Garbage Collection and Transportation Vehicles Parking and Maintenance

Depot with an area of more than 8,000 square meters and green coverage rate of over 90%. The design of the garden is closely integrated with the rolling landform of the surrounding mountains, making it quite natural. The garden is green and environmentally friendly and cherishes nature. Standing on the top of the hanging garden, one can see the infinite natural scene of the town in the distance, as well as the orderly and neat environment of the garden.

Tianziling Ecological Fruit Park is located in the southwest of the hanging garden. Established in April, 2012, covering a land area of 20,000 square meters, the park is planted with more than 1,000 fruit trees, such as orange, loquat, waxberry, peach, pearl, kiwi and grape and is integrated by sightseeing tour, popular science culture and leisure tastes. Tourists can not only pick fruits to experience the fun of harvest, but also taste special local foods, release stress, get close to the nature and experience happy and relaxing idyllic life. The fruit garden is also the Green Shooting Wedding Photography Base which is the first of its kind being constructed on the garbage mountain with shooting, sightseeing and traveling activities. It covers an area of about 10,000 square meters and has more than 100 scenic spots for wedding shooting, such as European Style Street, Tianjing Garden, Fantastic Space, and Swan Pond. The establishment of wedding base provides fashionable, individual and more environmentally-friendly choices for newly-wed couples and is a new highlight of wedding industry in Hangzhou and in China.

"Following the garbage to travel" is a tourism experience route featuring garbage treatment education and has won the Annual Communication Promotion Award conferred by the International Solid Waste Association. The route connects links of garbage treatment one by one in tandem to form narrative stories so that every visitor can feel close to the stories.

农夫山泉杭州千岛湖饮用水公司

1996年，一位浙商来到建德新安江，准备来此收购一家酒厂的他却被千岛湖的一湖好水吸引了目光，最终，收购"酒厂"变成了建立"水厂"，这个水厂就是农夫山泉的前身。这位商人便是创立了养生堂集团的钟睒睒先生，他在饮用水市场被纯净水占领的环境下慧眼识珠，开创了专注天然矿泉水的农夫山泉，也开拓了中国饮用水行业的新天地。

农夫山泉杭州千岛湖饮用水公司是中国饮料行业的十强企业，是集科研、开发、生产、营销于一体的农产品果汁饮料深加工企业，总部设在杭州。农夫山泉从不使用城市自来水，坚持水源地建厂、水源地灌装，目前在全国拥有8处优质水源地，总计18家工厂，是国内规模最大的天然饮用水公司。

农夫山泉的崛起，可以说是肇始于"农夫山泉有点甜"的广告词，这句广告词简单上口，容易记忆和传播。其实，这个广告词最早出自上海一个小朋友之口。1997年5月，农夫山泉选定上海为全国第一个试点市场。董事长钟睒睒亲自跑到上海调研市场，他在静安寺附近敲开一户居民家的房门，请他们全家品尝农夫山泉，家中的小朋友喝了一口，脱口而出："有点甜！"这就是"农夫山泉有点甜"的由来。

那么，是什么让农夫山泉有点甜呢？当然最重要的是水源地。

自始至终，农夫山泉都坚持"健康、天然"的品牌理念，从不使用城市自来水生产瓶装饮用水，只生产天然弱碱性的健康饮用水。钟睒睒认为，饮用水中应

该含有人体所需的全面、均衡、天然的矿物元素，并反对在水中添加任何人工矿物质。因此，优质的水源是农夫山泉的根本。农夫山泉在全国的八大水源地为浙江千岛湖、广东万绿湖、湖北丹江口、吉林长白山、新疆玛纳斯、四川峨眉山、陕西太白山、贵州武陵山。

农夫山泉有专职的水源勘探师，其担负起了寻找水源的重任。好的水源，往往隐藏在山深林密、人迹罕至的地方。为了在吉林寻找到一处顶级水源，水源勘探师近百次深入长白山腹地，徒步了上百公里的路程，冒着零下三十摄氏度的酷寒，进入长白山山麓的露水河国家森林公园之内，这次艰辛的寻找给农夫山泉带来了最新水源地：长白山莫涯泉。后来的检测表明，莫涯泉确实是举世罕见的低钠淡矿泉，水源来自30到60年前落在长白山上的积雪，经过地质矿层的渗析与溶滤，汇集成流，形成地下涌泉。

找到水源后，公司还要对水源进行长期的跟踪监测，以确保水质的稳定性。以峨眉山水源地为例，农夫山泉在峨眉山的西南寻找了整整6年，考察了上百个水源地，初步确定峨眉山是符合农夫山泉标准的水源地，又对之进行了2年的水质跟踪，才最终决定开发。

农夫山泉的八大水源地都位于国家一级水源保护区。比如千岛湖是国家一级水资源保护区，水域面积573平方公里，库容量178亿立方米。平均每立方米含沙量只有0.007千克，透明度达9米。千岛湖周边环境非常好，森林覆盖率达94%，没有污染。公司曾两次将水样送美国国家实验室检测，结果都合格。美国国家实验室是目前世界上最先进的实验室，它能检测270种物质，美国总统喝的水都是由这个国家实验室检测的。农夫山泉送去的水样其检测结果是270个指标全部合格。

农夫山泉坚持水源地建厂、水源地灌装的理念，所有生产过程均在水源地完成，以保障产品的天然健康品质，至今已在全国建有 18 座大型现代化工厂。农夫山泉拥有目前世界上最先进的生产线，从吹瓶、灌装到包装的整个生产过程全部采用微电脑控制，生产人员无须直接接触产品，确保产品不受任何污染。

经过 20 多年的发展，农夫山泉已建立起遍布全国的销售和配送网络，覆盖终端店商 110 万余家，由 31 个销售大区 423 个办事处的 4400 个经销商组成的销售网络将农夫山泉的产品及时地送到每一位消费者手中。

农夫山泉不只有矿泉水，还有其他饮料产品，如农夫果园、尖叫、维他命水/力量帝、水溶 C100、东方树叶、打奶茶等。

农夫山泉不仅对产品品质要求严格，对产品设计也有极高的追求。其中，农夫山泉高端水系列的包装设计历时 3 年，邀请了 3 个国家的 5 家顶尖设计工作室进行设计，经历 58 稿 300 余次设计后才最终定稿。这是中国企业借助世界智慧表达自己的价值理念的典范，面世以来，斩获多项国际包装设计大奖。

农夫山泉秉持着"天然、健康"的理念，二十年如一日，用心雕琢每一款产品，先后成为 G20 峰会、"一带一路"国际合作高峰论坛、金砖国家领导人厦门会晤的指定会议用水。2016 年，在杭州召开的 G20 峰会上，农夫山泉有 7 款产品入选为会议指定用水或饮料。由抚松工厂生产的玻璃瓶高端水是会议指定用水，除此之外，农夫山泉 380 mL 规格和 550 mL 规格瓶装水成为会议工作用水，4 L 水则是会议后厨用水。农夫山泉不仅证明了自身的优异品质，也代表着中国民族企业与民族品牌的形象，通过一瓶瓶"中国好水"向世界传递着"中国智慧"。

农夫山泉淳安生产基地位于淳安经济开发区，占地面积为 11 万平方米，其中绿化面积超过整个厂区的 40%，是一个名副其实的花园式工厂。公司从德国、法国、瑞士等国引进了当今世界一流的天然水生产线 4 条和热灌装饮料生产线 1 条，整个生产过程高速高效，实现了人机对话和自动监控，有效确保了生产过程中多个环节的产品质量。农夫山泉工厂内不仅机器科技化程度高，其他的设备也节能环保：厂房顶装的聚光板，一排排一列列整齐地排列着，晴天的时候聚光板能够很好地汇聚阳光，使得厂房内部十分明亮但不刺眼。

在淳安工厂的产品展示大厅里，可以看到有两个非常漂亮的展示柜：右侧摆满了农夫山泉天然水，每瓶水内都含天然矿物质元素，呈天然弱碱性，目前生产的规格主要有 380 mL、550 mL、750 mL，消费者可以根据不同需求和场合来挑选不同规格的水瓶；左边柜子上摆放的是农夫山泉公司生产的各种饮料。

近年来农夫山泉推出工业旅游活动，在农夫山泉淳安生产基地接待了许多消费者前来参观访问。基地拥有现代化的高科技设备、全自动化的生产工艺流程、全透明的旅游观光通道，消费者能欣赏到农夫山泉的整个生产过程，亲身体验农夫山泉天然水"有点甜"的独到之处。

Nongfu Spring Hangzhou Qiandao Lake Drinking Water Company

In 1996, a Zhejiang businessman went to Xin'an River in Jiande to purchase a winery and was amazed by the quality water of Qiandao Lake. He gave up the acquisition of "winery" and built a "water factory" instead. The businessman was Mr. Zhong Shanshan, the founder of Yangshengtang Group. As China's domestic drinking water markets were occupied by purified water at that time, Mr. Zhong was wise enough to initiate Nongfu Spring that focused on natural mineral water and thus opened up a new world in the drinking water industry of China.

Nongfu Spring Hangzhou Qiandao Lake Drinking Water Company is one of the top 10 enterprises in the beverage industry of China. Headquartered in Hangzhou, Nongfu Spring is an enterprise integrated by scientific research, development, production and marketing and is engaged in the intensive processing of agricultural products, juices and drinks. Nongfu Spring never uses urban tap water and insists on building factories and filling water at water sources. At present, it has 8 high quality water sources and 18 factories in China and is the largest natural drinking water company in China.

The rise of Nongfu Spring can be traced back to its simple and catchy advertising slogan "Nongfu Spring Tastes Sweet". Actually, the slogan was first uttered by a child in Shanghai. In May of 1997, Nongfu Spring selected Shanghai as its first pilot market in China. President Zhong Shanshan went to Shanghai to investigate the market by himself. He knocked at the door of a resident's house around Jing'an Temple and invited them to taste Nongfu Spring. After drinking a mouthful of the water, the child in the house blurted out: "It tastes sweet!" This is the very origin of the slogan "Nongfu Spring tastes sweet."

Then, why does Nongfu Spring taste sweet? It is because of its quality water source.

Ever since the beginning, Nongfu Spring has been adhering to the brand concept of "health and nature". It has never used urban water supply for producing bottled drinking water and insists on producing naturally alkalescent healthy drinking water. Nongfu Spring believes that drinking water shall contain comprehensive, balanced and natural mineral elements needed by human body and objects to adding any artificial minerals in water. Therefore, high quality water is essential to Nongfu Spring. So far the company has owned 8 water resources in China, including Qiandao Lake in Zhejiang Province, Wanlu Lake in Guangdong Province, Danjiangkou in Hubei Province, Changbai Mountain in Jilin Province, Manas in Xinjiang Autonomous Region, Emei Mountain in Sichuan Province, Taibai Mountain in Shaanxi Province and Wuling Mountain in Guizhou Province.

Nongfu Spring has a team of professional water source explorers. Good sources are usually hidden in dense forests and untraversed places. In order to find a top-grade water source in Jilin Province, water source explorers went into the depth of Changbai Mountain for nearly one hundred times and trekked for more than one hundred kilometers. They went into Lushuihe National Forest Park at the foot of Changbai Mountain in the bitter coldness of thirty degrees

below zero. The painstaking efforts paid off. They finally found the latest water source for Nongfu Spring—Changbai Mountain Moya Spring. Later, tests indicated that Moya Spring was actually a rare low-sodium light mineral spring in the world. The water is sourced from the snow fallen on Changbai Mountain 30 or 60 years ago. After penetration and filtration through geological seam, the water formed a stream and became a underground fountain.

After finding water sources, Nongfu Spring makes long-time efforts to trace and monitor water stability. Taking water sources of Emei Mountain for example, the company searched in the southwest of Emei Mountain for as many as 6 years and investigated more than a hundred water sources before tentatively determined that Emei Mountain was the water source that conformed to the standard of Nongfu Spring. After further tracing water quality for another 2 years, the company finally decided to develop it.

All of the eight water sources of Nongfu Spring are located in national first-grade water source conservation area. For example, Qiandao lake is a national first-grade water source conservation area with a water area of 573 square kilometers and a storage capacity of 17.8 billion cubic meters. The sediment concentration of the lake is only 0.007 kg/m^3 on average and the transparency is 9 meters. The surrounding environment of Qiandao Lake is excellent with forest coverage rate of up to 94% and is pollution-free. The company ever sent water samples to American National Laboratory to carry out tests for twice and was tested to be qualified. American National Laboratory is the most advanced laboratory in the world and can test 270 kinds of substances. The drinking water of American president is tested by the laboratory. The test results of Nongfu Spring showed that all the 270 indicators were qualified.

Nongfu Spring adheres to the product concept of building factory and bottle-filling water at water sources. The whole production process is completed at water sources to guarantee the natural healthy quality of products. Up to now, the company has established 18 large-scale modern factories all over China. Nongfu Spring owns the most sophisticated production line in the world. The whole production processes from bottle blowing and filling to packing are controlled by microcomputers. As production staffs don't have any direct contact with products, contamination of products is thus avoided.

After two decades' development, Nongfu Spring has established sales and distribution network throughout China with over 1.1 million terminal stores, 31 sales regions, 423 offices and 4,400 distributors, who work together to deliver Nongfu Spring products to each consumer in time.

In addition to mineral water, Nongfu Spring also turns out other drinks such as Nongfu Juice, Screaming, Vitamin Water/Powerful Emperor, Water-solution C100, Oriental Leaves, Matcha & Black Milk Tea, and so on.

Nongfu Spring has high requirements on products' quality and design. For example, it took 3 years and invited 5 top-notch design studios from 3 countries to design the packages for high-end water series. The design was finalized after 58 sketches and more than 300 design drawings. Nongfu Spring is a model of Chinese enterprises that express values with the help of world wisdom. Upon hitting the market, it has won numerous international awards for package design.

Sticking to the concept of "nature and health", Nongfu Spring was making painstaking efforts to consummate every item of product in the past two decades. It was the designated water brand for G20 Summit, Belt and Road Forum for International Cooperation and BRICKS Leaders Xiamen Declaration. In 2016, at the G20 Summit held in Hangzhou, 7 products of Nongfu Spring were selected as designated water or drinks. The glass-bottled high-quality water produced by Fusong Factory was the designated water for conferences.

In addition, the 380 mL and 550 mL red-bottle water were designated for the staff of the summit. The 4 L water was the designated water for kitchen use. Nongfu Spring represents the quality and image of Chinese national enterprises and national brands. Through bottles of high quality Chinese water, Nongfu Spring displays "Chinese wisdom" to the world.

Nongfu Spring Chun'an Production Base is located at Chun'an Economic Development Zone, covering a land area of 110,000 square meters. With green space of more than 40%, it is worthy of the name as a garden-style factory. The company introduces 4 world-class natural water production lines and 1 hot filling drink production line from Germany, France and Switzerland. The whole production process is speedy and efficient, and has realized man-machine dialogue and automatic monitoring to effectively guarantee products' quality in the whole production process. Nongfu Spring Factory has high mechanization and technicalization level and owns energy-conservative and environment-friendly equipments. The neatly arranged solar panels on the ceiling of workshops can well concentrate sunlight, making the workshops bright but not dazzling.

In the product exhibition hall of Chun'an Factory, there are two display cabinets. On the right, bottled natural water in various specifications are on display. Each bottle contains natural mineral elements and is slightly alkaline by nature. At present, products' specifications include 380 mL, 550 mL and 750 mL. Consumers can pick bottles of various sizes for different needs and on different occasions. The left cabinet displays the various drinks produced by Nongfu Spring Company.

In recent years, the company has launched a series of industrial tourism activities. Nongfu Spring Chun'an Production Base, with its modern high-tech equipment, completely automatic production flow, and transparent tourism sightseeing passages, has received many consumers and visitors. Consumers can see with their eyes the whole production process of Nongfu Spring and experience the unique feature of the natural "sweet" water.

康师傅梦想探索乐园

说起方便面大家一定不陌生，大家最耳熟能详的康师傅产品当然就是康师傅红烧牛肉面了。它是在四川红烧牛肉红油汤面的基础上研发而成的，是康师傅生产的第一包方便面，也是全世界迄今为止销量最高的方便面。

康师傅品牌经过多年的耕耘与积累，深受中国消费者喜爱和支持，康师傅方便面已经成为最受消费者喜爱的方便食品。想知道康师傅方便面一共有多少种口味吗？如果来到杭州康师傅梦想探索乐园进行一番考察，你就会发现，康师傅根据各地不同的口味已经研发出 200 多种不同口味的方便面。杭州钱塘江畔的康师傅梦想探索乐园，是康师傅斥巨资修建的全国第一座专为青少年儿童打造的工厂体验乐园。探索乐园用最先进的网络和视觉娱乐技术，为中小学生推出一个全新、生动、寓教于乐的神奇乐园。

康师傅梦想探索乐园由主体馆、美味专列、参观走廊三部分组成。作为全国首创的方便面体验馆，康师傅梦想探索乐园主要针对 6 ～ 12 岁的小学生群体，以梦想为主题，以科技为依托，以亲身体验为手段，以寓教于乐为目的，注重培养孩子们的探索能力，打破千篇一律的单纯游玩模式，通过游戏体验和科普参观的方式让消费者了解方便面的文化，有效传递出康师傅"健康、安全、美味、创新"的理念。

康师傅梦想探索乐园主体建筑面积近700平方米，活动面积1500平方米，包含梦想小剧场、童趣文化走廊、神秘通道、神秘厨房、环形放映厅等精彩互动

区，内部整体风格俏皮可爱。梦想探索乐园中探索活动丰富，设备先进，装修设计童趣十足，小火车、面条竖琴、好吃的方便面等，可以让小朋友们在玩得开心尽心的同时，增长知识和见识。外形可爱的康师傅美味专列车厢上还

图文并茂地展示了中国面文化从春秋到现代的发展历史。通过参观、游戏、学习、品尝、体验，参观者可以了解到康师傅在生产过程中繁复的工序和严格的安全检验标准，理解康师傅方便面的品牌理念和企业文化，引发儿童主动探索并分享其中的乐趣。

康师傅梦想探索乐园有几大亮点。首先，体验馆内利用低频蓝牙定位技术，根据参观者所处位置和场景，即时推送互动内容。小朋友可以通过具有"神秘透镜"功能的平板电脑，用虚拟视觉 VR 技术呈现出一个虚拟的梦想世界，发现只有在乐

园中才存在着的精灵生物。其次，特制的美味专列往返于主场馆与康师傅制面工厂之间，负责送每一位小朋友去探寻康师傅的工厂，亲见美味的方便面生产过程，包括混面、复合压延、蒸煮、淋汁、切断、整面、油炸、冷却、自动下碗、自动码箱等过程，带小朋友真实体验从挑选食材到制面，直至出厂的全过程。再次，梦想探索乐园里有专门为小朋友设计开发的多种高科技体感互动游戏，每款游戏的设置，都意在告诉小朋友，要实现梦想，需要通过自己的努力。在康师傅梦想探索乐园的最后环节，小朋友可以用丰富的食材，加上自己的奇思妙想，来亲自制作一份从内到外都只属于自己的独一无二的方便面带回家，送给小伙伴或父母，

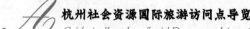
透过这个环节，希望告诉小朋友自食其、与人分享和交流的重要性。

康师傅梦想探索乐园作为杭州下沙区重点投资项目，已被评为下沙区青少年科普基地，未来将被打造成长三角区域亲子娱乐新地标。

Master Kong's Dream Discovery Land

Everyone is familiar with instant noodle. Master Kong's braised beef noodle is surely a household name. Originated from braised beef noodle with soup in Sichuan Province, it is the very first pack of Master Kong's and the top selling instant noodle in the world.

Master Kong has become one of the most popular instant food brand in China through years of hard work and development. It even has a large fan base in China. How many flavors are there? Having explored Hangzhou Master Kong's Dream Discovery Land, you would find out that Master Kong has more than 200 flavors. Master Kong's Dream Discovery Land, located along the Qiantang River in Hangzhou, is the first industrial experience park built for children and teenagers. The Discovery Land has an advanced network and a visual entertainment system, featuring a brand-new, vivid and educational wonderland.

Master Kong's Dream Discovery Land consists of a main pavilion, a gourmet railway, and a touring corridor. As a pioneering instant noodle experience center, it caters to primary school students from 6–12. Based on modern technology, the Discovery Land offers a great experience in both fun and educational way with dream as its theme. It lays emphasis on students' creativity and exploration competence and embodies the concept of "Health,

Safety, Delicacy and Creativity". Visitors can have a great experience in the Discovery Land by playing games in a scientific way.

Master Kong's Dream Discovery Land covers a floorage of nearly 700 meters. The 1500-square-meter active area has a lively and delightful interior decoration. It includes a wonderful interaction zone consisting of a dream theater, children's cultural corridor, mysterious tunnel, mysterious kitchen, ring-form video hall and so on. The Discovery Land has an advanced set of equipment, offering a series of activities. Its interior decoration covers a lively and delightful style. The little train, noodle harp and delicious instant noodle are exclusive fun and educational for children. On the wall of railway coach displays the history of Chinese noodle from the Spring and Autumn Period till today with illustrated texts and pictures. By visiting, game-playing, studying, tasting and experiencing, visitors become aware of the complicated production and safety-inspection and begin to understand Master Kong's brand culture. Children would therefore explore and share with friends and family so much fun.

Speaking of the highlights of Master Kong's Dream Discovery Land, there are quite a few of them. First, the experience center would post content for interaction according to visitor's position and scene through low-frequency Bluetooth. Children would get a virtual dream world through a tablet supported by VR tech with a mysterious lens, therefore discovering special creatures and spirits in it. Second, the Gourmet Railway runs between main building and factory. Each and every child would explore and have a view of Master Kong's noodle making process including flour making, calendaring, stewing, sauce putting, noodle cutting, noodle arranging, frying, cooling, automatic bowling up and packing. A complete working process from raw material, noodle making, to final packing is vividly demonstrated here. Third, children would find a lot of motion sensing games in the Discovery Land. Game settings aim to tell children

that it takes hard work to realize one's dreams. Finally, visitors could make an exclusive pack of instant noodle with the food materials they have seen in the Discovery Land and bring it back home to their friends or family. This activity aims to teach children to learn to be independent and willing to share and communicate with people.

As a key investment project in Xiasha District, Hangzhou, Master Kong's Dream Discovery Land has been rated as the Teenager Base for Science Education and will be made into a new landmark for parent-child entertainment in the Yangtze River Delta in the future.

梦想小镇

位于杭州城西的未来科技城，建城时间并不长，但其崛起迅速。那里人才云集、资本云集、项目云集，构建起了以新一代信息技术、健康医疗、现代金融服务、新能源、新材料为主导的产业集群，集聚了一大批优秀的科研项目，倍受社会各界关注。未来科技城的崛起，带动了周边一带的发展。于是，一座"梦想小镇"拔地而起，让天下"创客"纷至沓来。

梦想小镇不是一个行政意义上的镇，而是一个以大学生互联网创业为特色的小镇。它是杭州余杭区打造"区域核心链"式创业生态系统的重要展示，已然成为杭州市信息经济的重要平台。

梦想小镇落户在杭州余杭区中部的仓前镇，余杭塘河穿行而过。仓前是一个有着800多年历史的古镇，自古就有"江南粮仓，丝绸之府，鱼米之乡"之美誉，这里人杰地灵，民风淳朴。梦想小镇之所以落户仓前，在此地做互联网创业集聚区，是因为梦想小镇在空间上要有相对完整的小镇形态，可以进行疏密有度的空间布局，而仓前这个地方正好满足了这种要求。

作为梦想小镇一定要有文化背景作依托，古镇仓前有着非常深厚的文化沉淀，如章太炎国学文化、运河文化、蚕桑稻作文化等。除此以外，这里生态环境良好，和睦水乡、余杭塘河、西溪湿地、闲林港分布有序。另外，这里还靠近未来科技城、阿里巴巴淘宝城等现代化产业区。小镇还邻近浙江大学、杭州师范大学、浙江科技学院及小和山高教园区。总之，这里创业环境得天独厚，交通配套也非常完善。

　　梦想小镇涵盖了互联网创业和天使投资两大方面，其中：互联网创业方面重点鼓励和支持"泛大学生"群体创办电子商务、软件设计、信息服务、集成电路、大数据、云计算、网络安全、动漫设计等互联网相关领域产品的研发、生产、经营和技术（工程）服务企业；天使投资方面专门打造天使村，重点培育和发展科技金融、互联网金融，集聚天使投资基金、股权投资机构、财富管理机构，着力构建覆盖企业发展初创期、成长期、成熟期等各个不同发展阶段的金融服务体系。今天，梦想小镇已经成为传统和现代完美融合、充满活力的大学生创业小镇和基金小镇。

　　梦想小镇的迅速崛起，与整个未来科技城强有力的人才支撑、产业支撑、环境支撑、配套支撑息息相关。同时，也与仓前这个有着800余年历史的古镇有着千丝万缕的联系。

　　说到余杭仓前，杭州人都会想到这里不仅有美滋滋的掏羊锅，也是全国闻名的"四无粮仓"的所在地，还是国学大师章太炎的故乡。

仓前，原名灵源，自古就是著名的稻米之乡，粮源丰富，京杭大运河的支流余杭塘河横贯其中，运输便利。南宋朝廷看中其得天独厚的优势，于是就在灵源街之北建造了粮仓。粮仓于南宋绍兴二年（1132年）建成，有敖仓60间，仓厅18间，四周围墙250丈（1丈≈3.33米），颇具规模。古以南为前，灵源街位于粮仓前面，于是百姓就将灵源街称为仓前，久而久之，灵源的名称就自然地成了"仓前"。

现在的仓前粮仓坐落于仓前老街最东端的余杭塘河边，坐北朝南，由四栋单体建筑的粮仓组成，其中：两栋老仓建于清道光九年（1829年），距今已有近200年的历史；两栋新仓分别建于1957年和1963年，为原余杭县（现余杭区）第一批砖瓦结构沥青地坪的新式粮仓。1955年，仓前粮库的17个粮仓全部达到"四无"（无虫、无霉、无鼠、无雀）标准，被中央粮食部评为全国粮食先进单位。从此，仓前的"四无粮仓"成了全国学习的榜样。

2006年，余杭第一个中心粮库——仓前中心粮库建成并投入使用，粮库占地65亩（1亩≈666.67平方米），包括12座高大平房仓和器材库、办公楼等，仓容2.4万吨。仓前的历史上第一次有了现代化的高标准粮仓，为确保粮食储藏安全提供了更可靠的保障。

而今，这个高标准的粮仓又承担起了"大众创业、万众创新"的新重任，在设计者的"再创造"下，12个粮仓已变身为上下分层、连廊贯通的创新创业的"种子仓"，粮仓一下子就充满了时代感与节奏感。

余杭四无粮仓陈列馆

余杭四无粮仓陈列馆位于杭州市余杭区仓前街道仓前塘路88号，占地5.34亩，展馆面积近2000平方米，杂交水稻之父袁隆平院士题写馆名，于2009年7月8日正式开馆。陈列馆主要反映20世纪50年代老一辈余杭粮食人创建全国首批"无虫"粮仓和"四无"粮仓的光辉历史，是一座集粮仓文化、粮油文化和粮食廉政文化于一体的专业陈列馆，馆内完好保存的四栋"仓前粮仓"被列入第七

批全国重点文物保护单位。

余杭四无粮仓陈列馆共分五个展区：一是四无粮仓的创建和发展历史展区，二是粮食仓储历史展区，三是农耕文化展区，四是粮油知识展区，五是廉政文化展区。

章太炎故居

在京杭大运河的南端，余杭仓前的塘河畔，曾经诞生了中国近代民主主义革命家、思想家和国学大师章太炎。

章太炎（1869.1.12—1936.6.14），名炳麟，号太炎。生于斯长于斯的章太炎，自幼就接受祖、父辈的汉学熏陶和极其严格的排满抗清教育，青少年时期就立下以天下为己任的鸿鹄之志。23 岁时，章太炎离家赴杭求学，后投身于推翻清朝腐朽统治的运动中，开始了波澜壮阔的革命生涯和学术生涯，成为"一身而二任"

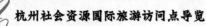
的革命家和学问家。

　　章太炎故居共四进一弄，占地面积为 688 平方米，建筑面积为 811 平方米，前三进为晚清建筑，第四进为民国初年所建，每进的主体均面宽三间、硬山顶，呈纵向逐层推高，并由东侧过弄前后贯通，各进间既相互关联又相对独立。

　　故居前三进为历史场景的再现，展示了章太炎先生青少年时期故居的风貌；第四进辟为展厅，以多种传统与现代相结合的手法展现了章太炎先生波澜壮阔的一生。

Dream Town

Zhejiang Hangzhou Future Sci-Tech City, which is located in the western part of Hangzhou, has been developing rapidly in recent years. Talents, capital, and projects swarm there, forming an industrial cluster that features information technology, health care, modern financial services, new energy and new materials. With a number of outstanding scientific research projects, the city has received much public attention. The emerging Future Sci-Tech city, a "Dream Town", has driven development of the surrounding area, creating a world of makers.

The Dream Town is not an administrative town, but a town characterized by college students' Internet entrepreneurship. As an important showcase of the "Regional Core Chain" entrepreneurial ecosystem in Yuhang District of Hangzhou, the town has grown into an important platform of Hangzhou's information economy.

Dream Town is settled in Cangqian Town which is in the middle of Hangzhou's Yuhang District, with Yuhangtang River zigzagging through. Cangqian is an ancient town with a history of more than 800 years, known as the "Granary of the south of the Yangtze River, home of silk, and the land of fish and rice". The locals there are carefree and honest. In its history, there emerged numerous outstanding talents. The reason why Dream Town is located in Cangqian and why it has been constructed into the Internet entrepreneurial cluster is that Cangqian has the exact dense layout that meets the spatial requirement of Dream Town.

A dream town is usually of highly cultural richness and Cangqian happens to enjoy profound cultural deposits, such as Zhang Taiyan's Guoxue (sinology) culture, canal culture, sericulture culture and rice-planting culture. In addition, Dream Town boasts nice ecological environment, with an orderly distribution of Hemu Wetland, Yuhangtang River, Xixi Wetland and Xianlin Port. Dream Town is also close to the Hangzhou Future Sci-Tech City, Alibaba Taobao City, Zhejiang University, Hangzhou Normal University, Zhejiang University of Science and Technology and Xiaoheshan Higher Education Zone. In short, Dream Town enjoys unique entrepreneurial environment and convenient transportation.

Dream Town involves two sections, namely, Internet entrepreneurship and Angel Investment. On the one hand, Internet entrepreneurship mainly encourages and supports "pan-university student" groups to establish enterprises on the research & development, production, operation and technical (engineering) service of products in Internet-related fields like e-commerce, software design, information service, integrated circuit, big data, cloud computing, network security and cartoon design. On the other hand, Angel Investment specially forges the Angel Village, focusing on the cultivation and development of sci-tech finance and Internet finance. It integrates Angel Investment Funds, equity investment institutions and wealth management institutions to construct a financial service system which covers the initial stage, growth stage and mature stage of enterprise development. Today, Dream Town has become a vigorous entrepreneurship town for college students as well as a fund town with the perfect combination of tradition and modernity.

The rapid rise of Dream Town is related to the powerful support from the Future Sci-Tech City in aspects like talents, industries, environment and supporting facilities. Cangqian Ancient Town, which enjoys a history of about 800 years, also contributes a lot to the development of Dream Town as its construction site.

Speaking of Cangqian town, Hangzhouese will immediately associate it with the delicious mutton hotpot, and the site of the "granaries with four frees" (pest-free, mildew-free, rat-free and sparrow-free), as well as the hometown of Zhang Taiyan (the great master of traditional Chinese culture).

Cangqian, formerly known as Lingyuan, has been a famous land of rice. With Yuhangtang River (a branch of Beijing-Hangzhou Grand Canal) traversing through, Cangqian enjoys convenient water transportation. Due to this, the imperial court of the Southern Song Dynasty (1127 A.D.–1279 A.D.) had granaries built in the north of Lingyuan Street. Completed in 1132, the granaries are of large scale with 60 grain bins, 18 halls and a surrounding fence of 250 *Zhang* (about 833 meters) in circumference. In ancient time, Nan (South) meant Qian (front). As Lingyuan Street was in front of the granaries, people called it "a street in front of the granary (Cangqian)", hence the name Cangqian.

The present granaries are located beside Yuhangtang River at the easternmost end of Cangqian Ancient Street. It faces south and is composed of four individual granary buildings, two of which were built in the 9th year of Daoguang reign of the Qing Dynasty (1829 A.D.) . The other two were built in 1957 and 1963 respectively, which were regarded as the first-batch new-style granaries in Yuhang County with brick-tile structures and pitch-surfaced terraces. In 1955, because all the 17 granaries in Cangqian Grain Depot were free of pest, mildew, rat and sparrow, they were appraised as a national advanced granary unit by the Ministry of Food of the People's Republic of China, becoming the model for all granaries in China.

In 2006, Cangqian Central Grain Depot, the first of its kind in Cangqian, was put into use. Covering a land area of 65 *mu* (about 43,333 square meters), it is composed of 12 large and high horizontal bins, equipment warehouses and office buildings, with a storage capacity of 24,000 tons. For the first time in history, Cangqian boasts modern and high standard granaries, which provide more reliable guarantee for the safety of grain storage.

Nowadays, these high-standard granaries have undertaken the new mission of "mass entrepreneurship and innovation". After "reconstruction" by designers, the 12 granaries are transformed into two-storied "seed granaries" for innovation and entrepreneurship and are connected each other by a corridor, making them modern and full of rhythm.

Exhibition Hall of Yuhang Four Granaries with Four Frees

The Exhibition Hall of Yuhang Four Granaries with Four Frees is located at No. 88, Cangqiantang Road, Cangqian Street, Yuhang District, Hangzhou, covering a land area of 5.34 *mu* with an exhibition area of about 2,000 square meters. The name of the hall was inscribed by Yuan Longping, an academician and the father of hybrid rice. Officially opened in July 8th, 2009, the exhibition hall mainly reflects the contribution of generations of Yuhang locals in building the first-batch pest-free granaries and four-free granaries in the 1950s. It is a specialized exhibition hall featuring granary culture, grain culture and uncorrupted grain administration culture. The four well-preserved granary buildings in the hall have been enlisted as the 7th batch key cultural relics

under national protection.

The Exhibition Hall of Yuhang Four Granaries with four Frees has five exhibition sections, namely, section of four-free granaries construction and development history, section of grain storage history, section of farming culture, section of grain and oil culture, and section of uncorrupted grain administration culture.

Former Residence of Zhang Taiyan

Zhang Taiyan, a democratic revolutionist, an ideologist and master of traditional Chinese culture in modern China, was born on the riverside in Cangqian of Yuhang at the south end of Beijing-Hangzhou Grand Canal.

Zhang Taiyan (January 12th, 1869–June 14th, 1936) (given name: Binglin; style name: Taiyan) was born and grew up in Cangqian. In childhood, he received rigorous sinology and anti-Manchuism education from his grandfather and father. As a teenager, he cherished the lofty ambition of serving his home country of China. At the age of 23, he left Cangqian to pursue study in Hangzhou. Later, he devoted himself to the campaign that aimed to overturn the ruling of decayed Manchu. His extraordinary revolutionary career and academic career forged him into a strong-minded revolutionist and dedicated scholar.

The Former Residence of Zhang Taiyan is a four-row and one-lane building, covering a land area of 688 square meters with a construction area of 811 square meters. The first three rows were constructed in the late Qing Dynasty, and the fourth row was built in the early period of the Republic of China. There are three rooms in each row, each of which has gabbled roofs that go upward longitudinally. All the rooms are independent of each other but

connected by a lane on the east side.

The first three rows of the building reproduce the scenarios of Zhang's childhood and adolescence. The fourth row has been turned into an exhibition hall, displaying the magnificent life of Mr. Zhang by combining both traditional and modern techniques.

社会文化
Social Culture

杭州学军中学

杭州学军中学是浙江省一级重点中学，始建于 1956 年。60 多年来，杭州学军中学已经发展成为一所现代化、国际化的全国知名高中，获得了浙江乃至全国同行的高度认可。

杭州学军中学初名杭州市第十四初级中学，先后更名为浙江师范学院附属中学、杭州大学附属中学，于 1970 年更于现名，1978 年被浙江省人民政府评为浙江省首批重点中学。60 多年来，变化的是校名，不变的是对学生的爱和对教育

的情怀。

　　在60多年的发展历程中，杭州学军中学始终以培养"领军人物"作为自己的办学目标，为社会培养了2万余名德才兼备的优秀毕业生。其中，有军事、科技、工程领域的领军人物，也有经济、体育、传媒、管理等方面的行业精英。

　　为了培养国内现代化的主力军和具有国际竞争力的领军人物，杭州学军中学积极推动课程改革。从1998年开始，杭州学军中学就贯彻"学教和谐，因人施教，发展个性，提高素质"的办学方针，开始了"弹性教学"学分制的研究，从重建课堂结构、试行学分制、活跃教学过程、实施多元评价、加强弹性辅导等五个方面入手，为每个学生提供适切的教育，满足不同潜质学生的发展需要。

　　在20世纪80年代，杭州学军中学的课程改革就蜚声全国。杭州学军中学提出了选修课、活动课与必修课三大板块并存的课程理念，改造选修课，增设活动课。

　　在建立更多丰富多元且国际化课程体系的基础上，杭州学军中学也注重课程实施的创新，逐步向"以学论教，因疑施教，先学后教，发展思维"转型。从2013年开始，杭州学军中学在全国率先进行"翻转课堂"的探索和实践，积极推动课堂教学方式的转变。同时，建立了"空中课堂"，打造"学军中学优质微课资源库"，为学生多样化的学习提供资源保障，为翻转课堂的进一步深化提供支撑。此外，杭州学军中学还积极推动教学模式的建设，包括：建设必修课课堂

的教学模式，引入研究项目，让学生在情境中提出问题，在思考和操作中研究问题，在合作探究中解决问题，在解决问题中提升学习能力；建设选修课"做中学、学中研、研中做"的教学模式，通过问题驱动、小组项目研究、小课题研究、小科学发明、程序设计擂台等形式，多样化实施课程，实现学科知识与操作技术点的对接融合，让学生以更加多样的学习方式巩固加深学科知识。

在开发优质课程的过程中，杭州学军中学建立了系统全面的资源保障体系。一是通过落实教师专业培训和健全校本研修制度，提升了校内教师的课程开发能力；二是利用杭州学军中学作为清华大学、北京大学、浙江大学、复旦大学、上海交通大学、中国美术学院等二十多所大学生源基地校的优势，邀请知名大学学者、教授、院士来校做讲座，开设学军大讲堂，丰富以学校文化和人文素养教育为主的主题课程；三是与校外教育机构合作，免费为学生提供知识拓展类课程和兴趣特长类课程，与一些职业高中达成战略合作伙伴关系，实现教师互聘、场地共用，开辟职业技能类课程教学基地，形成职业教育与实践课程群；四是利用国外友好学校资源，常年聘请外籍教师，开设着眼于国际交流和竞争的实践类课程。

杭州学军中学格外重视校园文化建设，以发挥隐性课程的指导作用。杭州学军中学始终把"培养什么样的人"和"怎么培养人"作为学校教育的主题，不仅关注学生学业的发展，更关注学生健全的人格、高尚的道德情操及正确的世界观、人生观、价值观和荣辱观的形成。学校教给学生的不仅仅是知识、技能，更是一种信念，一种做人的准则，一种支持学生足以走完人生历程的精神动力。

杭州学军中学在教职工队伍中，力求弘扬民主平等、宽松和谐，钻业务、尽责任、讲奉献的氛围，努力将学校的要求潜移默化地内化为每个员工的自我要求。在校本培训中通过"今天我们怎么做老师"的专题学习来提高教职工的思想素质。学校通过设置一年一度的"学术节"活动来引领教师从优秀走向卓越，其主题包括"做一个学术型的老师"和"做一个有思想的实践者"等。在课堂教学中，每个老师的言行举止、治学精神、为人处世等，都会对学生产生直接或者间接的影响，所以杭州学军中学提出要用教师的人格魅力去感染学生，在教师群体中形成"让奉献成为一种幸福""为学生播下精神的种子""创造性的智慧劳动""为尊严

而教，为荣誉而工作"的精神文化。

　　杭州学军中学为了培养学生有"世界眼光、民族情怀、创新精神、健全人格"，提出了八个 100%：100% 学生参加 60 天的志愿者活动，培养未来人才的国家意识、社会责任感和服务社会的能力；100% 学生参与研究性课题，激发学生的创新精神，培养学生的研究能力；100% 学生选择校本选修课，促进学生个性发展和多元化发展；100% 学生参与社团活动，培养自主管理意识和领导能力、团队精神和合作能力，实现人的社会化发展；100% 学生完成 100 个实验，在科学探究中验证和探究科学方法，培养科学精神、科学态度，提升动手能力和科学素养；100% 学生参加快乐体育，培养健康的体魄、承受挫折的能力和战胜困难的顽强意志，塑造积极进取、自强不息的精神品质，促进学生身心和谐发展；100% 学生"玩"上精彩艺术；100% 进入高等学府。

　　在过去的 60 多年岁月里，杭州学军中学已经在学生发展、教师专业成长、校园文化建设、课堂教学改革等方面取得了令人瞩目的成就。在收获成就的同时，杭州学军中学没有止步不前，而是继续酝酿新一轮更为彻底的改革，为提升每一位学生的核心素养做出更加积极的努力，为社会培养更多的卓越人才。

Hangzhou Xuejun High School

Hangzhou Xuejun High School is a provincial key middle school of Zhejiang Province. Since its establishment in 1956 for 60 years, Hangzhou Xuejun High School has been developed into a national famous modern and international high school and has been highly recognized in Zhejiang Province and even in China.

Hangzhou Xuejun High School was originally called Hangzhou No.14 Junior High School and was then renamed as Affiliated High School of Zhejiang Normal University and Affiliated High School of Hangzhou University successively. The present name came into existence in 1970. In 1978, it was assessed as Zhejiang First-batch Key Middle School by People's Government of Zhejiang. In the past 60 years, what was changed was only the name of the school, while the school's love for students and the devotion for education remained unchanged.

In the development course of more than 60 years, Xuejun High School has been adhering to the schooling goal of cultivating "leading figures" and has trained more than 20,000 outstanding graduates with professional competence and moral integrity. The leaders enjoy high prestige in the fields of military affairs, science and technology, engineering, economy, sports, media and management.

In order to cultivate the main forces for China's domestic modernization and the leading figures with international competitiveness, Xuejun High School actively advances curriculum reform. Since 1998, Xuejun High School has implemented the schooling policy of "harmonious studying and teaching, differential treatment in education, development of individuality and improvement of quality", and started the study of "flexible teaching" credit system. By restructuring classroom, trying credit system, activating teaching process, implementing multiple evaluations and strengthening flexible counseling, the school provides appropriate education to meet the different needs of students with different potentials.

In the 1980s, Xuejun High School was famous in China for its curriculum reform. The school proposed the curriculum concept of the coexistence of selective courses, activity classes and compulsory courses, reformed selective courses and additionally provided activity classes.

On the basis of establishing richer and more diversified international curriculum system, Xuejun High School also attaches importance to the innovation of the curriculum implementation, and it is gradually oriented to "evaluating teaching by learning, teaching based on questioning, teaching after learning, and developing thinking". Starting from 2013, Xuejun High School took the lead in China in the exploration and practice of "flipped classroom" to actively promote the transformation of classroom teaching mode. Moreover, it established "air classroom" to create "senior micro-curricular resource library" to provide resource guarantee for the diversified leaning of students as well as the support for the further deepening of the flipped classroom. In addition, Xuejun High School also promoted the construction of teaching modes, including building teaching models for compulsory classes, introducing research projects to allow students to ask questions in context, studying problems through

thinking and operation, solving problems through cooperation and exploration, and enhancing the ability of study in solving problems. Also, it ushered in the teaching mode of "learning from doing, researching during studying and doing in researching" for selective courses to allow diversified implementation of courses through question-driving, group project research, small project research, small scientific invention, and program design competition to realize the integration of subject knowledge and operational technology points, allowing students to consolidate and deepen subject knowledge in a more diversified learning mode.

In the process of developing quality courses, Xuejun High School has established a systematic and comprehensive resource guarantee system. Firstly, the school makes efforts to improve teachers' curriculum development ability by providing professional training and improving school-based research and training system. Secondly, based on Xuejun High School's advantage as the enrollment base of more than twenty universities, including such top universities in China as Tsinghua University, Peking University, Zhejiang University, Fudan University, Shanghai Jiao Tong University and China Academy of Art, the school invites famous university scholars, professors, and academicians to come to the school to give theme lectures concerning school culture and the cultivation of humanistic literacy. Thirdly, the school cooperates with off-campus education institutions to provide knowledge extension courses and sets up special interest courses for the students to learn freely. It also establishes strategic partnership with some vocational high schools to realize mutual recruitment of teachers and venue sharing, build vocational skills curriculum teaching base, form a vocational education and practice curriculum group. Fourthly, the school makes full use of the resources of its foreign friendship schools to hire foreign teachers all year round and provide practical courses focusing on international exchanges and competition.

Xuejun High School attaches great importance to the construction of campus culture and gives play to the guiding role of hidden curriculum. Xuejun High School always regards the target of the training and methods of training as the theme of the school education. It not only keeps an eye on the development of students' academic study, but also pays attention to students' sound personality, noble morality sentiments and correct outlook on the world, life, value, honor and disgrace. The school not only teaches students knowledge and skills, but also conviction, rules of conduct and spiritual motivation that support students to complete their life course.

Xuejun High School goes all out to create a democratic, equal, relaxing, harmonious, professional, responsible and dedicatory atmosphere among faculty, aiming to internalize the school's requirements as the self-requirement of each staff. Through the school-based training on the theme of "how to be a good teacher today" and the annual activity of "academic festival", the school effectively improves the ideological consciousness of the whole faculty. Thus school teachers grow from being nice to being outstanding. During teaching, teacher's words, scholarly spirit and behaving modes usually have direct or indirect impact on students. Therefore, Xuejun High School encourages teachers to inspire students with their "personal charm" which is characterized by "being happy in dedication", "sowing spiritual seeds among students", "laboring creatively and smartly", and "teaching for dignity, working for honor".

In order to cultivate students with "global vision, national sentiment, innovative spirit and sound personality", Xuejun High School advocates eight 100%, namely, make sure that 100% students participate in various volunteer activities for 60 days to cultivate their national awareness, social responsibility and ability of serving the society; make sure that 100% students

join in research projects to arouse their innovative spirits and enhance their research capabilities; make sure that 100% students choose school-based selective courses to promote their diverse personality development; make sure that 100% students are engaged in community activities, cultivating their self-management consciousness and ability in leadership, team spirit and cooperation; make sure that 100% students complete 100 experiments to verify and explore scientific methods in the scientific inquiry, cultivate scientific spirit and scientific attitude, and enhance hands-on ability and scientific literacy; make sure that 100% students get involved in sports to build up healthy body, forge strong will to overcome difficulties and foster the spirit of being positive; make sure that 100% students "play" with wonderful arts; make sure that 100% students are admitted by institutions of higher learning.

In the past 60 years, Xuejun High School has made remarkable achievements in students' development, teachers' professional growth, campus culture construction, and classroom teaching reform. Despite the achievements, Xuejun High School never ceases going forward. A new round of reform is under way to enhance the core literacy of students and to cultivate more talents for China.

杭州萧山南宋官窑艺术馆

公元1127年的"靖康之难"，徽、钦二帝被俘，北宋王朝覆灭，康王赵构登基，改年号为建炎，史称南宋。赵构成了南宋的第一任皇帝，也就是宋高宗。绍兴八年（1138），宋高宗在临安正式定都。在"靖康之难"中，宋朝宫廷的仪器法物及日常用器被金人席卷而去，初到浙江，对瓷器的需求量非常大，除了满足宫廷日常之需要，还要大量用作祭器。由于当时财力不足，铜料稀缺，无法大量重铸南下时已经失去的铜玉礼器，所以当时的祭奠活动，大多数祭器都从简用陶瓷器及木器。随着南宋政权的逐步稳定，"袭故京遗制"重设官窑的事情也被提到了议事日程之上。为了满足宫廷饮食、祭祀和陈设等方面用瓷的需要，朝廷在杭州凤凰山麓和乌龟山麓先后修建了两座官窑，一座叫"修内司官窑"，一座叫"郊坛下官窑"，专门用来为朝廷烧制高端瓷器。这两座官窑都是宋朝廷修建的，也就是宫廷御窑，所以史称"南宋官窑"。

官窑瓷是宋代五大名瓷之首，有"中国瓷器明珠"之称。南宋官窑制瓷工艺技术要求极其严格，器型由宫廷画师参照夏商周三代青铜礼器造型设计出图，经朝廷内府审核后，交宫廷制瓷技匠按照式样进行制作；以高铝、低硅、富铁的紫金土等原矿瓷料为主要成瓷原料，配制碱性草木灰釉料，三次以上施釉工艺，用采烧造阶段性温控工艺技术，烧造出具有"粉青釉色、紫口铁足、冰裂纹片、薄胎厚釉"四大艺术品质特色的南宋官窑青瓷。

这里的"粉青釉色"是指器物胎薄釉厚，釉层丰厚，色如美玉；"紫口铁足"是指器物口沿薄釉处呈现紫色，器物底足露胎部分呈褐色；"冰裂纹片"是指器物表面呈现如冰裂、蟹爪、梅花、蜘蛛网等形状的金丝纹线、银丝纹线和铁丝纹线；"薄胎厚釉"的"薄胎"是指产品的胎体经过多次修坯，多次素烧达到了极薄的胎体效果，"厚釉"是指产品釉层比普通陶瓷釉层要厚三倍以上。

南宋官窑烧制出来的瓷器在造型、装饰、釉色等方面都是按照宫廷设计式样进行制作的，具有浓厚的宫廷色彩。因为要满足宫廷的品质需要，南宋官窑对瓷器制作质量要求极高，在工艺上精益求精，在经济上不计成本。而且，官窑的产品只能供皇宫使用，具有非商品性、严禁民用的特点。

南宋王朝覆灭后，官窑被毁，工匠失散，技艺失传，有关官窑瓷器的原料、配方、烧制工艺等等，也无人知晓了。留传在世的南宋官窑瓷器大多是碎片残器，完整的据说不到百件，其中一些价值连城的被私人收藏着，也有一些分散陈列在不同国家的博物馆内，所以南宋官窑成品一直传世稀少。资料显示，目前仅存的南宋官窑瓷器在台北故宫博物院有70多件，收藏于故宫博物院的只有20余件，其他国内个别博物馆及欧、美、日的博物馆和个人也有零星收藏，中国民间的藏品极少。可以说，极高的品质、稀少的数量以及宫廷御用的神秘性决定了南宋官窑瓷器的珍贵。

1957年，周恩来总理在全国轻工业会议上，对恢复中国宋代名瓷做出重要指示。位列宋代名瓷之首的杭州南宋官窑瓷理所当然地成为重要的恢复内容之一。当时有个勤奋好学的年轻人叫叶国珍，17岁开始就和陶瓷打交道，从老家福建莆田来到金华陶瓷厂学做陶瓷。凭着一股钻劲，叶国珍很快掌握了陶瓷造型模具制作和日用陶瓷配方调配等技艺，并琢磨出实际生产中更简单、方便的成型工艺方法。1969年，叶国珍开始了研究恢复南宋官窑瓷的工作；1976年，他被调到萧山瓷厂，加入了由其哥哥叶宏明教授主持的南宋官窑名瓷恢复研究团队。为了破译"官窑密码"，叶国珍每天天刚蒙蒙亮，就从萧山住处出发，到西湖区乌龟山一带，在杂草丛中翻拨寻找，希望能找到一些有关南宋官窑的蛛丝马迹。功夫不负有心人，叶国珍终于找到了两座烧造南宋官窑瓷的龙窑遗址，并在遗址中发掘出用来进行岩相结构和化学组成分析的各种不同胎釉色瓷片。这些古瓷碎片是破译"官窑密码"岩相结构和化学组成的关键。叶国珍把瓷片分别送到上海和景德镇的陶瓷分析机构进行理化测试,取得了第一手研究资料。通过对南宋官窑遗址瓷片的分析研究,叶国珍和他的同事们终于攻克了制作原料、制瓷配方、成型技艺和烧造技术的难关。

在试验制瓷原料的一年时间里,叶国珍带着锄头和麻袋,差不多跑遍了杭州主城区及萧山、富阳、余杭、临安周围的大小山岭。通过试验和对比,他确认乌龟山郊坛下南宋官窑窑址附近的紫金土,是制作烧造官窑瓷器最重要的原料。

找到了紫金土制瓷原料后,叶国珍开始研究胎釉配方和制作烧造技艺。在漫长的试验过程中,一窑瓷器要连续烧制 17 个小时才能出炉,因此,不管白天还是黑夜,酷暑还是寒冬,只要窑中有试验品,叶国珍都一直在现场观测,观察火焰,记录炉温,确定氧化与还原时间,分析各种不同辅助原料对南宋官窑瓷器四大特征的影响。他前前后后共选用了 10 多种辅助材料,通过上千个配方试验与调整,

72 道制瓷工序的优化与提升，2000 多次品质特征窑烧试验，终于一步步迈向成功之路。

除此之外，叶国珍还亲自到国外博物馆观看南宋官窑实物，查阅资料。在不断的摸索和反复的实践中，终于在 1978 年成功仿制烧制出南宋官窑瓷器。在仿南宋官窑瓷国家级鉴定会上，专家一致认为叶国珍研究恢复成功的官窑瓷与南宋官窑瓷相比，无论是内在质地还是外观形象，都完全一致，达到了以假乱真的地步，而且制作烧造工艺技术更加合理科学。收藏家评价叶国珍的作品是南宋官窑品质和青瓷艺术精华相结合的结晶，是现代南宋官窑的经典之作，并称他为"中国碎瓷王"。

为了让广大民众欣赏到南宋官窑瓷的艺术魅力，帮助广大的陶瓷收藏爱好者更好地鉴赏南宋官窑瓷这一历史珍宝，专业展示南宋官窑瓷的民营艺术馆——杭州萧山南宋官窑艺术馆于 2005 年正式落成并对外开放。叶国珍担任南宋官窑艺术馆馆长。

这是杭州市第一家以南宋官窑青瓷文化艺术为专题并常年免费开放的专业性艺术馆。艺术馆占地面积 5332 平方米，展馆面积 3600 平方米，内设展览陈列厅、藏宝阁、贵宾厅和品茗居，还设置了馆藏系列、古瓷复制品、现代抽象系列以及

传统定制等四大区块，充分展示了杭州南宋官窑青瓷文化艺术的独特魅力。

　　杭州萧山南宋官窑艺术馆内还有国内第一家南宋官窑瓷艺体验中心，公众可以通过参与技艺体验活动，了解南宋官窑青瓷文化的历史价值，培养和提高对南宋官窑古瓷的鉴赏力，体验艺术创作的魅力。

Hangzhou Xiaoshan Southern Song Dynasty Official Kiln Museum

In 1127, the Jingkang Incident took place. Emperors Huizong and Qinzong were captured by the Jin army. This marked the end of the era of the Northern Song Dynasty. Zhao Gou, later known as Emperor Gaozong, changed the title of his reign into Jianyan, and became the first emperor of the Southern Song Dynasty. He reestablished the capital at Lin'an (now Hangzhou) in southern China in 1138. During the Jingkang Incident, many royal properties were looted by the Jin army. When the imperial court settled in Zhejiang during its early stage of development, there was a high demand for porcelain, not only for the court's daily use, but also for worship ceremonies. Due to the shortage of bronze and other financial resources, it was impossible to remake the bronze and jade vessels lost in the long journey. Therefore, most ritual vessels at that time were made of porcelain and wood. After the political environment became stable, the system of inheriting traditions from the old generations on reestablishing the official kiln was put on the agenda. In order to meet the imperial needs of porcelain dinnerware, ritual vessels and decorations, the court built two official kilns on Fenghuang (Phoenix) Mountain and Wugui (Tortoise) Mountain. One was named Xiuneisi Official Kiln, and the other was named Jiaotanxia Official Kiln. Both kilns provided porcelain for the court

exclusively. As built and owned by the Song Dynasty itself, these kilns are called "Southern Song Dynasty official kilns".

The official kiln is one of the Five Famous kilns of Song Dynasty, known as the "Pearl of Chinese Porcelain". Official kilns had very strict criteria in the porcelain making procedures. Royal painters designed the body based on the bronze vessels of Xia, Shang and Zhou Dynasties. After verified by the imperial court, the design was handed over to porcelain technicians to form the body. The technicians used Zijin clay, which was abundant in aluminum and iron and low in silicon, as the raw material, added with alkalic plant-ash glaze. After being glazed for more than three times and through temperature control stages, the fired porcelain then displayed four precious artistic features: fine hues of the celadon color, a purple-colored mouth and a rust-colored bottom, cracked-ice texture, and a thin clay body with a thick layer of glaze.

Fine hues of the celadon color reflect the translucent color created by the thick glaze on the thin body. The purple here refers to the color of the thinly-glazed ware mouth, and the rust means the brown color of the un-glazed bottom. The cracked-ice texture here refers to the patterns highlighted with gold, silver or iron that are likened to ice cracks, crab claws, plum blossoms and spider's webs. Besides, the clay body is trimmed and fired repeatedly to ensure extreme thinness. The glaze, on the contrary, is usually three times thicker than normal porcelain glazes.

The porcelain by official kilns accorded with the imperial design in terms of its shape, decoration and glaze. To meet the demand of the royal court, the official kilns were meticulous in the processing, regardless of the cost, to ensure the quality. Moreover, the official kilns only supplied products for the royal court. Commercial and civil use were strictly prohibited.

When Southern Song Dynasty was brought to an end by Yuan Dynasty, official kilns were destroyed one after another. The artisans and their porcelain making techniques were lost in the history. The remaining porcelain from Southern Song Dynasty official kilns are mostly in fragments. Undamaged items are found no more than one hundred. Some of the valuable ones have been collected privately, and some are exhibited in different countries. Very few have been handed down completely. It is documented that Taipei Palace Museum has around seventy items in collection, while Palace Museum only holds about twenty. Other items are scattered in museums in China, Europe, America, Japan and are owned by some private collectors overseas. Very few remain in civil China. Therefore, the porcelain from Southern Song Dynasty official kilns become very precious especially for its high quality, rarity and imperial mysteriousness.

During the National Light Industry Conference in 1957, Premier Zhou Enlai announced the revitalization of Song Dynasty porcelain. Hangzhou Southern Song Dynasty official porcelain, ranking top among Song Dynasty porcelain, was definitely one of the focuses. At that time, Ye Guozhen, a clever and diligent young man, started working on porcelain since he was 17 years old. He left his hometown Putian in Fujian and came to Jinhua in Zhejiang to learn ceramics. He was passionate about ceramics, so he quickly mastered the techniques of modeling and formulation. Moreover, he refined the forming techniques to improve production efficiency in practice. In 1969, he embarked on reviving the Southern Song Dynasty official porcelain. He was assigned to Xiaoshan Porcelain Factory in 1976 and took part in the porcelain restoration team led by his brother, Professor Ye Hongming. Aspiring to decode the official kiln secrets, Ye Guozhen got up early every day to search for any traits hidden inside the Wugui Mountain in Xihu (West Lake) District, a long way from his home in Xiaoshan District. Where there is a will, there is a way. Eventually, he found two Long (Dragon) Kiln relics where Southern Song Dynasty official porcelain was produced. He also found porcelain body and glaze fragments for petrographic configuration and chemical components research. These fragments, as the key to uncover the official kiln secrets, were sent to ceramics research institutions in Shanghai and Jingdezhen for physical and chemical analysis. Having undertaken plenty of research and obtained first-hand data, Ye Guozhen and his colleagues finally worked out the formulation, forming and firing techniques to combat problems in porcelain making.

For a whole year, Ye Guozhen, carrying his hoe and bag, went into the mountains in Hangzhou downtown, Xiaoshan, Fuyang, Yuhang and Lin'an, to search every corner for raw materials. After lots of experiment and comparison, he drew the conclusion that the Zijin clay near the Jiaotanxia Official Kiln relic under Wugui Mountain was an important material for official porcelain making.

With the raw materials in hand, Ye Guozhen started to look into the formulation techniques of the body and the glaze. It usually took 17 hours to fire a chamber of porcelain. However, as long as there were articles in the chamber, Ye Guozhen stayed with the chamber day and night to observe and document the data. He analyzed the effect of different supplementary materials on the four characteristics of the Southern Song Dynasty official porcelain. More than ten materials were tested one after another. Thousands of experiments were performed to modify the formula. Seventy-two porcelain making procedures were optimized. More than two thousand chamber experiments were carried out to check qualitative characteristics. These efforts all paved the way to his success. Moreover, Ye Guozhen went overseas to study porcelain exhibits in person and read piles of historic documents. After continuous exploration and practice, he finally succeeded in imitating Southern Song Dynasty official

porcelain in 1978. During the national appraisal meeting, scholars agreed that Ye Guozhen's porcelain resembled the original Southern Song Dynasty official porcelain both in texture and appearance. Even experts could not distinguish it from the genuine. Ye Guozhen's producing techniques, however, were even more scientific than the ancestors. Collectors appraised that Ye Guozhen's porcelain possessed the quality of Southern Song Dynasty official kilns and the essence of celadon porcelain arts. It was a classical artwork in modern times. Ye Guozhen himself, thereafter, had obtained the title–King of Fragmented Porcelain.

Offering more people a chance to appreciate the porcelain of Southern Song Dynasty official kilns, Hangzhou Xiaoshan Southern Song Dynasty Official Kiln Museum was open to the public in 2005. Ye Guozhen was the curator.

This is the first free and professional Museum themed in Southern Song Dynasty official celadon porcelain. The Museum covers an area of 5,332 square meters. The exhibition halls take up 3,600 square meters. The Museum encompasses exhibition department, treasure department, VIP department and tea tasting department, and four sections including the collection section, antique replica section, modern series section and traditional customization section. It fully demonstrates the unique charm of the celadon porcelain from Hangzhou Southern Song Dynasty official kilns.

The Museum has a pioneered experience center for official kiln porcelain in China. Inside the center, visitors can get to know the historical values of celadon porcelain culture through practice. The experience activities are expected to cultivate people's aesthetics of the Southern Song Dynasty official porcelain. It also gives people an opportunity to experience the fascination of creating artworks.

塘栖谷仓博物馆

位于杭州北部的塘栖镇始建于北宋，是一个历史悠久的古镇，明清时为"江南十大名镇"之首，也是乾隆皇帝七下江南时来过数次的古镇。

说起塘栖，杭州人首先想到的是枇杷，枇杷似乎成了塘栖给杭州人的定情物。杭州人买枇杷要问是不是塘栖的，不是塘栖的似乎就不是正宗的，看来塘栖枇杷已成了一个果类高端品牌。

塘栖镇距杭州市市中心约 20 公里，著名的京杭大运河潺潺流淌，穿镇而过，商业街夹岸而建，使其成为苏、沪、嘉、湖的水路要津，历朝历代，塘栖均为杭州市的水上门户。明清时期，塘栖镇富甲一时，贵为江南十大名镇之首。塘栖有着深厚的文化积淀，文人辈出，书香传世。塘栖文物遗产众多：广济长桥、郭璞古井、乾隆御碑、栖溪讲舍碑、太史第弄、水南庙等等。可以说，塘栖是一座古镇，同时也是一座新城。虽然历经岁月沧桑，但是她的魂和根还在，并且充满了生机和活力。当旅游者置身于塘栖老街风情特色街区，面对林林总总的糕点、小吃、乡土风味的餐饮、民宿，目不暇接的古迹、景点的时候，总有一种流连忘返的感觉。

在塘栖众多文物、景点中，最为经典的应该是那块乾隆御碑。1985 年，塘栖镇文化站进行文物普查时，在广济桥北岸的水北街耶稣堂西侧、原杭州府水利通判厅遗址内，发现了这块御碑。乾隆御碑碑高 3.35 米，宽 1.4 米，厚 0.5 米；碑身添有碑额，镌有双龙抢珠石刻，高 1 米，宽 1.5 米；碑身下有碑座，碑座出土高度 1.1 米，宽 1.8 米，厚 1 米。碑上有正文 429 字，落款 10 字，碑文四周

镌有云龙纹，据考证为中国国内现存最大的御碑。1751 年乾隆皇帝南下考察江苏、浙江、安徽三省交纳皇粮情况，查得江苏、安徽两省积欠钱粮数额巨大，而浙江省则未积欠钱粮。为表彰浙江省圆满完成钦定任务，乾隆皇帝大笔一挥，蠲免浙江省地丁钱粮 30 万两，并将"圣谕"刻在石碑上，告昭天下，晓谕官民。

今天，在御碑南面运河畔耸立着一座高大的牌坊，来来往往的游人都会在这里驻足留影。但是，游人们可能不知道，皇上在这里留下"圣谕"，其实不仅仅是单纯地表扬浙江省没有积欠钱粮，主要还是想把浙江当作样板，要各地向浙江看齐，完成朝廷规定的漕运任务。当然完成漕运任务的关键之一，就是要管理好运河两岸的谷仓。因为谷仓内的粮食不仅能够保障封建王朝最基本的粮食需求，而且也是应对战争、饥荒、自然灾害等意外情况的必需品，同时还可以对市场供需起到调节作用。

京杭大运河自开凿以来，其命运始终与中国的漕运制度相伴相生。漕运制度是中国古代一项重要的经济制度，是利用水道调运粮食的一种专业运输制度。在漕运这部历史连续剧中，运河两岸的谷仓必然起着非常重要的作用。江南运河两岸的谷仓曾经是历史上米市、仓储和码头装卸业等经济业态发展、繁荣的实体见证，也是研究中国传统仓廪建筑的实物例证，是运河文化体系的有机组成部分，对后人完整、深刻地揭示、挖掘和理解运河历史文化内涵起到了重要的作用。

塘栖是杭州漕运的一个起点和终点，明清时期，这一带布满了大大小小的谷仓。民国期间的塘栖是著名的米市。

为了挖掘运河漕运文化和谷仓之间的关系，阐述谷仓在人类生存与文化进步中的重要地位，利用农耕文化和仓储文化元素，营造兼具传统文化内涵和时代精神的休闲场所，在塘栖乾隆御碑附近，原来老字号米厂兴良

米业的储粮地，后来也是国家储备粮基地上，建立了塘栖谷仓博物馆。

塘栖谷仓博物馆是一座下沉式建筑，展馆面积 6500 平方米，分为两层。它是一座以谷仓为展示主题的"充满泥土和谷物气息的现代化博物馆"，完整地保留了乾隆十六年（1751）的御碑和兴良米业厂、原国家储备粮仓的老建筑。塘栖谷仓博物馆通过挖掘漕运文化和谷仓之间的关系，叙述谷仓和农业起源、文明诞生、城市兴起、人类战争与和平的关联，鲜

明地阐述了谷仓在人类生存与文明进步中的地位。

"民以食为天"，博物馆以历史进程顺序为线索讲述了谷仓的由来、谷仓的变化，通过文字、画面、模型、多媒体等展示了先秦至近代的与中国谷仓相关的文物，包含东汉时期的"陶仓罐""瓷魂瓶"、清代纸质"漕粮纳税执照"等。还以我国不同少数民族及世界各地谷仓模型展现了不同的谷仓建筑特色。此外，介绍了五谷相关知识并展示了旧时期的农具。

塘栖谷仓博物馆以浓墨重彩之笔，详细地介绍了我国谷仓的发展历史。"粮食系国脉，民心定乾坤"，历朝历代，粮食问题都是头等大事，所以统治者都对粮食种植和储存表现出高度的重视。塘栖谷仓博物馆以模型和文字叙述了中国古代的太仓为国之大命。太仓是保证皇室生计与国家机器运转而设立的中央粮库，是王朝政治最重要的物质基础。

　　游客在这个博物馆里可以发现，中国粮食专仓储备制度开始于春秋战国之际，到秦代进一步发展，到了西汉时期兴盛起来，发展至隋唐时期规模宏大，号称"资储遍于天下"。中国古代军仓的重要作用也在这里有叙述。"兵马未动，粮草先行"，粮食储备是古代打仗最重要的物质保障，运粮线路过长历来是兵家大忌，一般军队都有固定粮仓作为后勤保障，这就是军仓。军仓大多数设立在驻防处或者屯田处。

　　通过参观可以发现，由于环境不同，各地在长期的实践中发明出了各种各样的谷仓。从历代明器与画像砖上的谷仓形象看，谷仓的种类众多、式样繁复。从地域看，北方多土木结构，多雨潮湿的江南地区盛行干栏式结构，四川一带有用编竹夹泥做成的墙壁。在形式上，早期的谷物贮藏多采用在地下挖窖的方式，称为"仓窖"，地面式通常称为"仓廪"。形制上则有方形或长方形的房式仓、高大的楼阁式仓以及干栏式仓。在粮食储量太大时，还会有临时的露天仓。

　　在塘栖谷仓博物馆里，游客可以看到不同形态的展品都是依据当时的现实谷仓做成的模型，观众可以了解当时的储藏环境、储藏水平。中国人所说的"民以食为天"，正是以农户的囤满仓实为基础的。为了使储存的粮食受到更好的保护，各族人民发挥了自己的聪明才智，发明了许多防止储粮因潮湿霉变或鼠患虫灾受损的方法。

　　谷仓是农耕时代流落在乡村中最具代表性的建筑之一，这些圆形的或长方形的建筑不仅给人们带来信心与宽慰，也让空气中弥漫着谷物与干草混合的清香。

这种气息是如此的温馨和亲切，以致当它们因时过境迁而成为明日黄花时，仍然深深扎根在人们的记忆中挥之不去。

在这里，参观者也可以了解到中国当代粮食储藏的现状。中华人民共和国成立后，国家十分重视粮食的储存和粮仓的建设。从 20 世纪 50 年代中国第一个"四无粮仓"在浙江余杭诞生到如今，全国共有粮库 58000 多个，仓房类型繁多，包括平房仓、筒仓、楼房仓、圆仓、浅圆仓等。

参观塘栖谷仓博物馆会发现谷仓这个朴实无华的建筑物与人类社会的发展是如此密不可分，它在人类生存与社会发展中扮演了非常重要的角色：农业的起源、文明的诞生、城市的兴起、人类的战争与和平均与谷仓息息相关。

Tangqi Granary Museum

Located in the north of Hangzhou, the town of Tangqi was built up in China's Northern Song Dynasty. In the Ming and Qing Dynasties, it stood at the top of the ten most famous towns in the south of Yangtze River. Qianlong (1736–1795), one of the emperors in the Qing Dynasty, visited Tangqi several times during his seven visits to the south of the Yangtze river.

Speaking of Tangqi, Hangzhou locals would immediately think of loquat, which seems to have become the token of Tagnqi to Hangzhou. Whenever Hangzhou people buy loquats, they would ask whether they are from Tangqi, which have long been acknowledged as a high-end type of its kind. If not, they may think the loquats are not authentic enough.

Tangqi is about 20 kilometers away from the downtown of Hangzhou. The world-renowned Beijing-Hangzhou Grand Canal goes through it with commercial shops lined on both sides of the river. Its convenient location has made it the hub of cities like Suzhou, Shanghai, Jiaxing and Huzhou for ages. Tangqi reached its heyday in the Ming and Qing Dynasties and was renowned as the top ten towns in the south of Yangtze River. Tangqi, boasting rich cultural literacy, has cultivated a number of famous scholars. Many cultural heritages like the Guangji Long Bridge, Guo Pu Ancient Well, Qianlong Imperial Tablet,

Qixi Stele in honor of the establishment of a lecture hall for Tangqi intellectuals, Taishidi Lane, Shuinan Temple can be found here and there. Tangqi is old in history and new in vigour. With the passage of time, Tangqi has gone through ups and downs, but her root is still stuffed with vitality. Strolling along the old streets in Tangqi, tourists are sure to feast their eyes on a variety of pastries, snacks, local foods and drinks, B & B (a bed and breakfast), historic relics and scenic spots. They are always too delighted to be homesick.

Among all the cultural heritages and scenic spots mentioned above, the most classic one is the Qianlong Imperial Tablet, which was found in 1985 during the census of cultural relics conducted by Tangqi Cultural Station. Qianlong Imperial Tablet is 3.35 meters high, 1.4 meters wide and 0.5 meter thick. The top of the tablet, which is 1 meter high and 1.5 meters wide, is engraved with stone inscriptions of two dragons snatching a pearl. Under the body of the tablet is a pedestal, whose unearthed height is about 1.1 meters high, 1.8 meters wide and 1 meter thick. There are 429 words in the tablet's text and 10 words in the tablet inscription. The inscription is surrounded by dragon cloud pattern. According to textural research, this tablet is by far the largest of its kind that is still in existence. In 1751, Emperor Qianlong went south to inspect the royal tax payment of Jiangsu, Zhejiang and Anhui only to find that Jiangsu and Anhui owed a large amount of money and grain and only Zhejiang didn't. In order to commend Zhejiang for its mission accomplishment assigned by imperial edict, Emperor Qianlong exempted 300,000 thousand liang (a traditional unit of measurement in ancient China) land of tax. The imperial edict was inscribed on the tablet for the general public to know and follow.

Today, tourists usually stop and take pictures at the torii in the south of the imperial tablet by the Grand Canal. They probably don't know that the imperial order mentioned above is not only to praise Zhejiang people

for their contribution to the imperial court in imperial tax payment, but also to set Zhejiang as a model, encouraging other provinces to complete the task of water transport of grain to the imperial court. Then one of the keys to completing water transport of grain is to properly manage the granaries on both sides of the canal because the granaries can not only guarantee the basic need of food in China's feudal dynasties but also provide a necessity for coping with unexpected wars, famines, natural disasters and other unforeseen circumstances. Meanwhile, it can also regulate market demand and supply.

Ever since the digging of the Grand Canal, its fate has been closely connected with China's water transport of grain, which is an extremely important economic system in ancient China. It is a kind of professional transportation system. Granaries on both sides of the Canal witnessed the boom of rice market, storage and wharf loading and unloading, thus playing an important role in the history of water transport of grain. They are also the material proof of China's traditional granary building and an integral part of canal cultural system, revealing and understanding the historical and cultural significance of the Canal.

In the Ming and Qing Dynasties, Tangqi, as the starting and ending point of the water transport of grain in Hangzhou, abounded with granaries. In the period of the Republic of China, Tangqi served as a famous rice market.

In order to explore the relationship between canal transport culture and granaries, elaborate the key position of granaries in human survival and cultural progress, create a leisure venue with both traditional cultural connotation and the spirit of age by manipulating the elements of farming culture and storage culture, the Tangqi Granary Museum, which was the grain storage site of an old rice firm, Xingliang Rice Firm, later the national grain reserve base, was set up near the Qianlong Imperial Tablet.

The Tangqi Granary Museum is a sunken architecture, covering an exhibition area of 6,500 square meters with two floors. The museum is a modern barn-themed one with tangible smell of soil and grain. The museum fully preserves the Qianlong Imperial Tablet (in the year of 1751) and original sites of Xingliang Rice Firm as well as the old building of the former national reserve base. By exploring the relationship between the culture of water transport of grain and granary, The Tangqi Granary Museum narrates the connection between granary and agricultural origin, the birth of civilization, the rise of city, the relations between wars and peace, hence expounding the status of granary in human survival and civilization.

As the old saying goes, "Food is the first necessity of people".The museum tells about granaries' origin and changes from the pre-Qin period to modern times via texts, pictures, models, multi-media and so on, displaying granary-related relics which include Taocang Tank and Cihun Bottle in Eastern Han Dynasty, and "Grain Tax Payment Licenses" in Qing Dynasty. The museum goes on to show the different granary models in China's ethnic minorities and around the world. In addition, it introduces the corn culture and the farm tools in old times.

The Tangqi Granary Museum elaborates on the history of China's granary development. As foodstuff is of vital importance to the state and the people, the issue of grain cultivation and storage has always been the top priority for each dynasty or government. Taking this into consideration, the museum introduces with words and models that Taicang (Imperial Granary), which was built to ensure the smooth operation of imperial families and the country as a whole, and was the material basis of a country.

Visitors can find in this museum that China's grain reserve system began in the Spring and Autumn Period, developed in the Qin Dynasty, flourished in

the Western Han Dynasty, and boomed in the Sui and Tang Dynasties where granaries are set up all over China. Ancient China's military granary was also worth mentioning here. As "Food and fodder should go ahead of troops and horses", grain reserves remained to be the most important material guarantee for wars in ancient times. Long grain transport route is a major taboo for the army. Therefore, armies had fixed military granaries established in garrisons and farming-storing areas for logistics support.

In the museum, visitors will find different styles of granaries that suited different conditions. For instance, wooden granaries were popular in the north of China while in the south, stilt-styled granaries were commonly seen due to the wet weather. In Sichuan, which is located in the southwest of China, there were many granaries with walls made of mudded bamboo clips. Speaking of granary's shape and structure, grain was stored in underground cellars, known as "Cang Jiao", or in above-the-ground granaries know as "Cang Lin". There are square or rectangular, pavilion-style and stilt-style granaries. In case of too large amount of grain, outdoor granaries were set up temporarily.

In the granary museum, different granary models that are made in light of the genuine granaries in China's ancient times are on display, through which visitors can get to know the storage environment and storage level in a particular period of time. The Chinese old saying "Food is the first necessity of man" can only be realized with full storage of granaries. In order to prevent granaries from being damaged by dampness, mildew or infestation by rats and insects, people of all ethnic groups have developed many methods.

Granary is one of the most representative buildings in rural areas during the agrarian era. The round or rectangular granary buildings not only brought confidence and comfort to life, but also filled the air with the fragrance of grain and hay. The smell was so warm and lingering that even today, people cannot

get rid it from their memories.

Here in the museum, visitors can also learn about the current situation of grain storage in China. After the founding of the People's Republic of China, the government attaches great importance to the construction of granaries. In the 1950s, China's first "Granary with 4 Frees" (pest-free, mildew-free, rat-free and sparrow-free) came into operation in Yuhang, Zhejiang Province and by now, there are 58,000 granaries all over China, among which there are horizontal bins, silos, multi-storied granaries, round-shaped granaries, squat silos and the like.

A visit to the museum is to find the inseparable relationship between plain-looking granaries and social development. Granaries reflect the origin of agriculture, the birth of civilization, the rise of cities, as well as war and peace.

杭州之江文化创意园——凤凰·创意国际

青山翠谷间，铺陈着一大片青草地，20余米高的巨型水泥圆筒，错落起伏着，现代化的景观电梯分别依附在老式的水泥建筑旁，墙上斑驳的红漆标语却又仿佛把人拉回到20世纪70年代，这就是植根于废弃水泥厂内的创意园区——凤凰·创意国际。

凤凰·创意国际是由原国营双流水泥厂改建而成的。因水泥行业是高污染高能耗产业，在发展经济的同时也给当地的环境带来了一系列的消极影响，所以，政府通过回购水泥厂，"腾笼换鸟，筑巢引凤"，采用综合改造和全面拆建相结合

的方式，来发展文化创意产业。

环绕在大片的山林绿地之中的凤凰·创意国际犹如一处世外桃源，它是杭州目前创意园区中产业配套环境最好、环境品味最佳、物业品质最独特、建筑形态最丰富、改造投资最高的国际性创意产业示范园区。人们往往一走进凤凰·创意国际，就被它极富个性的建筑风格所吸引。当年的生产设备——巨型水泥圆筒和空中传输长廊，都被完好地保留了下来。灰色外墙充满阳刚气质，墙上的红漆标语让人难辨哪些是原来的，哪些是设计师的"仿旧作品"。环顾整个创意园区，随处可见特色建筑与创意雕塑，处处都展示着它独特的风采和魅力。

创意园内亮点很多。如被称为"文创资本粮仓"的空间，原先是堆放矿石的仓库，现已成了文创项目投融资服务平台。已经有100多家创投机构进入创意园，为前来逐梦的文创年轻人才解决低资产、难评估、弱担保、难融资等问题。

原来水泥厂的水泥筒熟料库如今已经改造成了咖啡吧，被称为"创意圆桌"，发起人是德籍华人、中国美术学院的客座教授何见平先生。这里是园区企业头脑风暴的场所，每个周末园区都会牵头做一期创享沙龙，创意者们会自发地在这里

聚会、交流、学习。

走出咖啡吧可以看到另外一个亮点：一个被称为"盒子美术馆"的独立玻璃空间。每一个盒子相当于一个小的展览空间，里面放置一件来自造否空间艺术家的艺术品，并且每个月会根据不同的节日或商场活动做一次更换。盒子美术馆颠覆了传统意义上的美术馆，它将那些"高大上"的艺术品搬到了人们日常生活当中来展示，以此来提高大众的艺术鉴赏力。

蔡志忠文化馆也落户在这里，文化馆占地120平方米，内部纯白色的装修基调体现了蔡志忠漫画一贯清新淡雅的风格。

离开蔡志忠文化馆，前面就是凤凰芳草地商业街，这里是园区的配套商业设施，是一个集餐饮、艺术互动、展览和活动于一体的艺术综合体。时尚的环保设计、永续发展的理念和丰富多元的艺术氛围构成了凤凰芳草地的独有特色，为每一位到访者带来充满新意的独特体验。凭借浓郁的艺术氛围与多元的商业文化休闲综合优势，如今的凤凰芳草地商业街已成为杭州风格时尚与高品质的新复合生活板块。

凤凰·创意国际的企业的建筑设计都很有特色，如外文书刊的阅览室、大承景观设计的办公室、仟果工艺品的仿真食品展览厅等等。另外，园区咖啡吧有中西餐供应，有与山居青年旅社和三星级宾馆，进行体育运动可以去网球场、篮球场、健身房。

凤凰·创意国际最热闹的时期，是每年 4 月底的中国国际动漫节、10 月的杭州文博会以及 12 月的圣诞节期间。暑假则是青少年培训的密集期，一些国际化、专业性的平面设计、影视后期特效、漫画、室内设计培训等会在这里开班。

领略了历史与艺术感兼具的水泥筒办公空间后，沿着彩虹小道可以进入凤凰创意大厦。作为创意园的延伸，凤凰创意大厦集办公、会议、酒店、购物、展览等功能于一体。

进入大厦，首先看到的是 3000 平方米的艺术展厅，这里曾举办过许多大型的活动展览，如中国国际动漫节峰会、开园海报展等等。

走出展厅，映入眼帘的是大厦内最具设计感的一个办公空间。这里是设计师

创意驻栈中心，同时也是生活艺术讲堂。驻栈中心，借鉴于艺术家驻留计划，它是一个重塑设计师工作模式和思考方式的能量中心，是一个创意发电站，吸引着来自全国各地乃至全球的设计师。它同时也是创意设计产业人才深度交流的平台，可以把中国创意、中国创造转化成中国生活，实现产业对接与融合。

在创意大厦的最东面是配套的艺术精品酒店——凤凰艺馆。酒店犹如一个艺术博物馆，传递着创意、创新的理念，于山水间悉心雕琢 80 余间艺术精品客房，尽显商务与创意的激荡、时尚与艺术的交汇。

凤凰·创意国际园区主要旅游点有：

蔡志忠文化馆：这是我国第一家以蔡志忠名字命名的文化馆，馆内有最全的蔡志忠动漫书籍和丰富的蔡志忠手绘图及衍生产品，包括《世说新语·菜根谭》《庄子》《唐诗·宋词》等限量版经典作品。

法蓝瓷展厅：台湾法蓝瓷以璀璨的颜色、优雅的造型和深厚的文化内涵深受人们的喜爱。该处是法蓝瓷在浙江的展示、销售中心，展出法蓝瓷各系列产品。

大学生科技创意中心：面积 3500 平方米，现有 60 多家大学生创业团队，涉及影视广告、壁画雕塑、首饰服饰、网络、工艺品等领域。一楼还展出园区企业的特色创意产品，如限量版设计文具、工艺品、迪士尼 3D 文具、台湾树脂挂件、仿真食品等。

凤凰创意馆：以创意格子铺的形式，为小微文创企业、大学生创业团队提供成果转化平台，馆内商品琳琅满目，80% 产品为独一无二的原创设计。

凤凰手工课堂：组织各类手工达人，教市民进行 DIY 活动，包括制作纯银饰品，学做陶艺、布艺、插花、编织等。

都市版画公社：由都市快报联合中国美术学院版画系共同打造，是面向都市大众的艺术创作、展示、学术交流平台。

孰料设计品咖啡店：是目前最时尚的"1+N"式的潮店，"1"是咖啡美食，"N"是德国、意大利、泰国、韩国和中国香港等 20 多个国家和地区的不同品牌创意产品。聚集东西方受人热捧的产品，或摩登，或简约，或优雅，或复古，打造老百姓买得起的潮牌店。

　　与山居青年旅社＆来点咖啡吧：一幢砖红色小楼，宽敞的庭院，构成了温馨的来点咖啡吧，旁边是沿山而建的与山居青年旅社。

　　凤凰创享沙龙：每周举办一期，一般在周五下午，邀请文创名人、政府职能部门代表、中国美术学院教师等作为嘉宾参加，主题涉及创业指导、行业交流、政策解读、项目对接、艺术展览、生活娱乐、周末影院、党建互动等。

　　昔日破旧的水泥厂变身为文创新基地——凤凰·创意国际，恰如一只涅槃的凤凰，在文创产业的春风中，迎来了重生。

Hangzhou Zhijiang Cultural Creative Park—Phoenix Creative

Among green vales and hills lies vast meadow with over 20-meter-high cylinders undulating. Modern panorama elevators are attached to the cement building whose walls are filled with mottled red slogans, bringing people back to the 1970s. This is the place where a deserted cement plant was turned into the creative industry district—Phoenix Creative.

Phoenix Creative was reconstructed from the state-owned Shuangliu Cement Plant in the past. Due to the fact that cement industry belongs to the high pollution and high energy consumption industry, the cement plant contributed much to the local economy while it also led to a series of negative influence to the local environment. Therefore, the government bought back the cement plant and changed the way of planning layout by means of combination of integrated transformation and overall demolition and construction to develop cultural creative industry.

Phoenix Creative, surrounded by large forests and meadows, is an international creative industry demonstration district like a land of idyllic beauty, which has the best supporting industry environment, the best environment standard, the highest quality property, the most diversified shape of buildings, the highest reconstruction investment among the creative districts in Hangzhou at present. Walking into the Phoenix Creative, people will be intoxicated by its unique architectural style. The past production equipment — the giant cement cylinders and the conveyor corridor in the air, are well preserved. The grey outer walls are of virile style. It is difficult to tell the real part from the designer's artificial part of the red paint slogans. Looking around the whole creative district, there are distinctive buildings and creative sculptures, showing its unique charm and grace.

The entire creative district has many highlights. Firstly, the so-called "cultural and creative capital stockroom" space, which used to be a stockroom to pile up ore, now has become the investment and financing service platform for cultural and creative programs. More than 100 creative investment facilities have entered the creative district, which solved the problem of low assets, assessment difficulty, weakness in guarantee and financing difficulty for young creative and cultural talents who came here to achieve their dreams.

The past cement cylinder clinker warehouse has been reconstructed into a coffee bar which is called the "creative table" sponsored by Mr. He Jianping, a German Chinese and the visiting professor of China Academy of Art. This is the place where enterprises within the creative district brainstorm. A salon is held on weekends for creative people to spontaneously gather around, communicate with each other.

When you walk out of the coffee bar you can see another highlight of the park: the so-called "box gallery" which is a unique glass space. Every glass box, equal to a small exhibition space, is placed inside a piece of artwork from the artists of Zaofou Space. The artworks will be replaced every month according to different festivals or shopping mall activities. The glass box gallery topples the traditional meaning of gallery and presents high-end works of art to ordinary people in an effort to enhance people's artistic literacy.

Cai Zhizhong Culture Center is also located here. The floor space of the cultural center is 120 square meters, with pure white color decoration showing the fresh and elegant style of Cai Zhizhong's comics.

After leaving the Cai Zhizhong Cultural Center, there's Phoenix Grassland Commercial Street that lies ahead. It is the supporting commercial facility which is an artistic combination of catering, art interaction, exhibition and activities. The fashionable green design, the concept of sustainable development and diversified art atmosphere contribute to the unique characteristics of the Phoenix Grassland, bringing unique experience to all visitors. By virtue of the comprehensive advantage of the rich art atmosphere and diversified commercial culture, the present Phoenix Grassland Commercial Street has become a new quality composite living area of Hangzhou fashion style.

The enterprises' design style of Phoenix Creative are quite distinctive in terms of the reading room of foreign books and periodicals, the office designed by Dacheng Landscape Company, the simulated food exhibition hall of Qianguo Artware Company and the like. Besides, the coffee bar of the district provides both Chinese food and western food and Yushanju Youth Hostel and three-star hotel service. Tennis court, basketball court and fitness center are available for people to play sports.

Every year, the park witnesses the China International Cartoon and Animation Festival is held in the end of April, the Hangzhou Cultural Expo in October and the Christmas Day in December. Many intensive training courses are held during summer vacation and class sessions like international and professional graphic design, special effects film post-production, cartoon, and interior design are available within the park.

After experiencing the cement cylinder office space with history and art, you can enter Phoenix Creative Mansion along the Rainbow Path. As an extension to the creative district, Phoenix Creative Mansion provides office, meeting, hotel, shopping and exhibition services.

When you walk into the mansion, a 3000 square-meter art exhibition hall is presented in front of you. This is the place where many large-scale activities and exhibitions are held, including China International Animation Festival Summit and Poster Exhibition of the Creative District Opening, etc.

When you walk out of the exhibition hall, the best designed office space in this mansion stands in front of you. This is the place where living art is taught and designers' inspiration burst. The Zhuzhan Center, drawing lessons from Artists in Residence, is an energy center to remold designers' working patterns and way of thinking and also a power plant producing originality, attracting nationwide or even worldwide designers. It is also a platform for deeper communication among talents from creative design industry, which paves the way for the transformation of China Creativity and China Making to China Living, making the joint integration of industries possible.

Lying at the east side of the Creative Mansion is an affiliated art boutique hotel—The Phoenix Art Hotel. The hotel is like an art museum featuring creativity and renovation, where 80 art boutique guest rooms are well designed and arranged.

The main tourist attractions within the Phoenix Creative are as follows.

Cai Zhizhong Culture Center: The first culture center named after Mr. Cai Zhizhong in China. The center has the most complete collection of comics, hand-drawings and derivative works of him, including limited edition of his classics like *A New Account of the Tales of the World—Caigentan* (Tending the Roots of Wisdom), *Zhuang Zi*, *Tang Poetry and Song Poems*.

Franz Exhibition Hall: Franz from Taiwan is famous for its bright color, elegant structure and profound cultural connotation. The hall is the exhibition

and sales center of Zhejiang displaying all series of Franz products.

Undergraduate Science & Technology Creativity Center: There are over 60 undergraduate entrepreneurial teams working in the 3500-square-meter center, covering the fields of television advertising, mural and sculpture, jewelry and clothing, Internet and handicraft. The first floor of the center also exhibits featured creative products like designed stationery of limited edition, artworks, Disney 3-D stationery, resin accessories from Taiwan and simulated food model.

Phoenix Creative Pavilion: The lattice shops here provide platforms for small cultural and creative enterprises as well as undergraduate entrepreneurial teams to commercialize their achievements. The pavilion is filled with various products, 80% of which are of original design.

Phoenix Handwork Classroom: Craftsmen in different fields are invited here to teach citizens to do DIY handicrafts like silver jewelry, pottery, fabric art, ikebana and knitting.

Metropolis Printmaking Community: It is a platform co-created by City Express and China Academy of Art for art creation, exhibition and academic communication among the general public.

Shuliao Designed Product Coffee Bar: It's by far the most trendy "1+N" fashion shop. "1" means coffee or delicious food while "N" means different brands of creative products from more than 20 countries or areas like Germany, Italy, Thailand, South Korea, and China Hong Kong, etc. This is also a hot place to try affordable and well-designed creative products in modern, simple, elegant or vintage styles.

Yushanju Youth Hostel & Laidian Coffee Bar: The coffee bar is a redbrick house with a spacious courtyard, right next to Yushanju Youth Hostel built against a mountain.

Phoenix Creativity Sharing Salon: The salon is held every Friday afternoon, inviting celebrities of cultural creativity, government representatives and teachers from China Academy of Art to have themed activities such as guidance of business starting, communication meeting of business, policy interpretation, project cooperation, art exhibition, life and entertainment, weekend movie theatre, and Party-building.

The shabby cement factory in the past has now been turned into a cultural creativity basis. Phoenix Creative, like a phoenix from nirvana, is ready to step into boom and prosperity.

杭州市社会福利中心

中国已经进入了国际公认的老龄化社会，过去，四世同堂的家庭模式为"老有所养"提供了家庭保障，而随着人口流动的加快、居民居住条件的改善以及民众家庭观念的慢慢改变，儿孙满堂、子孙绕膝的情景在中国越来越少见了，所以，养老已成为刻不容缓需要解决的社会问题。

就目前中国的现状看来，老人进入敬老院养老是一种值得推荐的方法，特别是一些敬老院推行人性化服务，利用先进的 IT 技术手段，开发面向居家老人、社区、机构的互联网系统平台，提供实时、快捷、高效、智能化的养老服务，借助"养老"和"健康"综合服务平台，满足老年人多样化、多层次需求。这是中国人养老的新趋势，也是目前中国养老产业发展的一个重要方向。

杭州市社会福利中心在这方面进行了有效的尝试并逐渐向社会推广，深受休养员家属的赞许。

杭州市社会福利中心位于杭州市拱墅区和睦路，于 1999 年 11 月成立，占地面积 4 万平方米，建筑面积 53933 平方米，按国家级福利院标准建设，环境清雅幽静，其绿化率在 60% 以上，是一所具有园林化格局的休养中心。福利中心目前拥有 1500 张床位、1300 多名休养员、240 多名员工。以自费寄养为主，为老年人提供生活照料、医疗护理、人文关怀等服务，具有生活、医疗、康复、文化、娱乐等多种功能，是一家集养老整体护理、老年病康复、个案康复护理、养老护理培训于一体的知名养老机构。

　　福利中心共设休养楼7幢，除1幢为特护楼外，其余6幢休养楼都是身体健康、有自理能力的休养员的生活楼。生活楼的房间大多为双人标间，同时根据休养员的不同需求提供套间、单间等其他户型。每幢休养楼均配有空调和电梯，每个房间都有彩电、电话、独立洗手间、紧急呼叫器等。每层楼至少配有一名护理员，为休养员打扫房间、送水，提醒休养员按时用药等等。此外，休养员可根据自身的不同需求，购买相应服务，如让服务员帮助买饭、购物、洗衣、做个人卫生等。

　　整个福利院内景观丰富、绿化场地配置合理有序，以带状、块状等形状绿地为主，园林植物以乔木、灌木、花卉、草坪、地被植物等为主，环境布置科学合理而又赏心悦目。楼与楼之间回廊相连，错落有致。庭院内道路畅通无阻，无障碍通道、电子门禁、呼叫系统、监控系统等现代化设施一应俱全。休养员们在绿树成荫、鸟语花香的环境里阅读学习、休息锻炼、散步聊天、接待访客，就如同在自家的庭院中一样舒适自在。

　　在餐饮方面，福利中心一直致力于帮助休养员在摄取丰富营养的同时，享受到美味的食物。食堂每周为有不同护理需求的老人提供三种菜单，对特护老人提供三种套餐供选择，让休养员自由选择搭配购买。为了让老人买得放心，吃得安心，福利中心还多种措施并举打造"阳光厨房"。

　　为了丰富休养员的精神生活和物质生活，福利中心内还设有专为老年人提供

服务的健身房、阅览室、棋牌室、台球室、乒乓球室、网球场、羽毛球场、电脑室、休闲区、塑胶运动场、超市等设施。福利中心因人、因地制宜，举办兴趣小组活动，举办嘉年华、运动会、美食节等。在生活自理区，积极鼓励休养员自发开展英语、书画、摄影、古诗词等小组学习，丰富老年人的精神文化生活，提升养老品质。福利中心为休养员提供的沟通和交流机会，让老年人之间的相处更加融洽。福利中心还设置法律援助点，每月 18 日为法律援助日，由专业律师为老年人免费提供法律咨询、遗嘱代书等服务。

随着休养员年龄的增长，对医疗服务的需求与对护理服务的需求都在逐渐增加，针对这一实际情况，福利中心始终坚持"医养结合"的新型养老模式，以"持续照顾"的养老服务理念为指导，尽可能使休养员在舒适的居住环境中得到持续的养老服务照料，实现老有所养，老有所医。福利中心还与周边的医院合作，通过公开招投标，签订合作协议，由医院派医生、护士进驻福利中心，为休养员提供医疗服务。福利中心的医疗设施比较齐全，医务室分为医生诊疗室、复健活动室、针灸理疗室、输液室及药房等几个部分，可提供健康咨询、健康检查、疾病诊治等服务。

福利中心还积极链接社会医疗资源，努力为休养员带来优质医疗服务。如与一些医院开展双向转诊合作，根据老人病情需要，进行转院诊治；也有大医院的名医定期来福利中心开展义诊服务，举办有关健康、营养、自我护理方面的讲座。福利中心还在特护楼专设医疗服务区，开设门诊、输液、家庭病床、康复理疗等项目，为特护休养员提供规范化和个性化服务。

福利中心根据入住需求对老人进行生理疾病、心理智能、生活能力的评估后，

提供分类等级服务。针对休养员的不同需求，提升服务的精细化、专业化、个性化水平。对休养员的护理具体分为三个层次：首先是针对身体基本健康的休养员，一般以自理为主，让休养员自己做些力所能及的事情，福利中心适当提供帮助；其次是提供专项护理，根据需要，为休养员提供从休养环境的设计到生活护理、膳食、医疗、专项护理方面的个性化服务，借助手工劳动、广播操等丰富特护休养员的生活；再次就是为失智老人提供失智护理服务。

福利中心融入居家式人性化服务理念，失智服务是福利中心的重点服务项目之一。在失智护理专区，专门设计和营造了特殊的模式和环境。区域内配备感应门、背景音乐、彩绘墙面、特殊门房标识、特殊活动室。杭州市社会福利中心是杭州首个引入智能看护机器人的养老院。机器人具有语音视频、伺药提醒、娱乐互动等多种功能，为老人提供智能看护、亲情互动等服务。这些都旨在为老人提供更加方便舒适、个性化的智能养老环境，逐步实现一键式、一站式和智能化养老服务模式。

福利中心的发展，得到了各级政府和领导的关怀，国家、省、市领导相继到福利中心来视察、调研，指导福利中心工作步入科学发展轨道。福利中心还与一些高校和慈善机构开展合作，建立学生实践基地，组织志愿者来福利中心对失智老人实施关爱活动。

2014年，由福利中心牵头，组织成立了杭州市养老服务协会，对进一步规范杭州市养老服务业的发展起到了积极的作用。

今天，杭州市福利中心已经成为全省养老机构护理人员和管理人员的示范培训基地，先后获得了"全国模范养老机构""示范型养老机构""敬老文明号"等光荣称号。

Hangzhou Social Welfare Center

China has entered an internationally recognized aging society. In the past, the family model of four generations living under one roof provided family guarantee for the elderly. However, with the acceleration of population mobility, improvement of living conditions and gradual change of people's concept for family, the scenes of having children and grandchildren around the knees have become rare. Therefore, provision for the elderly has become a social problem that needs to be solved urgently.

As far as the current situation in China is concerned, living in gerocomiums is a solution recommendable for the elderly. Especially, some gerocomiums provide humanitarian service and implement advanced IT technology to develop an Internet platform system for the elderly, communities and institutions. They provide instant, efficient and intelligent elderly care services to meet the diversified and multi-level needs of the elderly by relying on the "ageing" and "healthy" integrated service platforms. This is a new trend of elderly care in China and an important direction in the development of China's elderly care industry.

Hangzhou Social Welfare Center has made effective attempts in this area and is highly praised by the families of the people under recuperation in the center.

Located on Hemu Road of Gongshu District, Hangzhou Social Welfare Center was established in November of 1999 according to the national standard for welfare house, covering a land area of 40,000 square meters, and a construction area of 53,933 square meters. Having elegant and quiet environment and a greening rate of more than 60%, it is a garden-style recuperation center. At present, the welfare center owns 1,500 beds, about 1,300 recuperators and more than 240 members of staff. It is based on self-funded foster care and provides daily care, medical care, humanistic care and other services for the elderly. With the functions of living, medical treatment, rehabilitation, culture and entertainment, it is a famous elderly care institution integrated by comprehensive care for the elderly, rehabilitation from geriatric diseases, individual rehabilitation nursing, and nursing care training.

The welfare center totally has 7 recuperation buildings. Except for one special nursing building, the other six buildings are living buildings for healthy recuperators with self-care ability. Most rooms of the living building are double-bed standard rooms. There are also suites, single rooms and other room types available to meet the different needs of recuperators. All buildings are equipped with air-conditioners and elevators. Each room is installed with color TV, telephone, separate toilet and emergency calling device. Each floor has at least one attendant who cleans room, delivers water for recuperators, and reminds recuperators to take medicine on time. In addition, the recuperators can purchase services from attendants according to their different needs, such as buying food, shopping, laundry service and personal hygiene.

The whole welfare center has rich and varied natural landscape with appropriate allocation of greenbelts mainly in the shape of belts and blocks. The garden plants include arbors, shrubs, flowers, lawns, and ground-covered plants. The environmental layout is scientific, reasonable and pleasing to eyes.

The buildings are well-proportioned and are connected by corridors. The roads in the courtyard are accessible without obstruction. The center is completed with wheelchair accessible passage, electronic access control, calling system, monitoring system and other modernized facilities. The recuperators can read, study, rest, exercise, walk, chat, and receive visitors in the center with shady trees, twittering birds and fragrant flowers, and will feel as comfortable and leisurely as if they were in their own courtyard.

In terms of food and beverage, the welfare center has been dedicating to making sure that the recuperators take delicious and nutrient foods. Each week, the canteen provides three menus for the elderly with different needs to choose from and offers three a la carte dishes to the elderly who need special care. In order to make the elderly feel at ease in buying and eating, the welfare center has built a "sunshine kitchen".

In order to enrich recuperators' spiritual and material life, the welfare center also provides gym, reading room, chess and card room, billiard room, table tennis room, tennis and badminton court, computer room, recreation area, rubberized tracks, supermarket, and other facilities for the elderly. The center also organizes interest group activities, carnivals, sports meetings and gourmet festivals. In self-care area, recuperators are encouraged to study English, painting, calligraphy, photography and ancient poetry in groups to upgrade their spiritual and cultural life. In addition, the welfare center creates opportunities to ensure the communication between recuperators for them to get along well with each other. Also, the welfare center provides legal service on the 18th day of each month, on which professional lawyers will provide legal consultation, allograph of wills and other services for free for the elderly.

As recuperators' demand for medical and nursing services gradually rise with the increase of age, the welfare center adheres to the endowment

mode that combines medical treatment with pension service. Guided by the pension service concept of "continuous care", the center tries best to make recuperators receive continuous care in a comfortable environment so that the elderly are properly looked after and treated. The welfare center signs cooperative agreements with surrounding hospitals through open bidding. The hospitals assign doctors and nurses to enter and stay in the center to provide medical services for the recuperators. The welfare center has complete medical facilities, which include doctor's clinic, rehabilitation room, acupuncture physiotherapy room, transfusion room and pharmacy, providing medical and health consultation, disease diagnosis and treatment services.

In addition, the welfare center is actively linked to social medical resources and goes all out to provide high quality medical services for recuperators. For example, it carries out two-way referral cooperation with some hospitals, and transfers the elderly to another hospital for treatment according to their needs. In addition, famous doctors of large hospitals are invited by the welfare center to provide free clinic services and give lectures on health, nutrition and self-care. Also, the welfare center sets up special medical service area in the special-care building, offering outpatient service, intravenous infusion, family bed, rehabilitation and physical therapy and other services, and providing standardized and personalized services for special-care recuperators.

The welfare center provides classified services after assessment of the physiological maladies, mental intelligence, and living ability of the recuperators based on the center's occupancy needs. In light of the different needs of recuperators, the center makes endeavors to guarantee the refinement, professionalism and individuality of its services. The care for recuperators is done at three levels. Firstly, for basically healthy recuperators, the center makes them take care of themselves and encourages them to do things within their power while providing proper assistance. Secondly, for recuperators that need special care, the center provides personalized services ranging from the design of recuperation environment to life care, diet, medical care, special care, and enriches their lives through having them do some manual work and broadcast gymnastics. Finally, for old demented people, the center provides dementia care services.

The welfare center advocates home-like humanitarian service concept. Dementia care service has been one of the key services of the center. The dementia care area is equipped with induction door, background music, painted wall, special concierge signs and special activity rooms. Moreover, the center is the first gerocomium of its kind in Hangzhou to introduce intelligent robots for care service like audio video, medication reminder and entertainment interaction, creating a more convenient, comfortable and personalized intelligent living environment. With these, one-click and one-stop intelligent care service for the elderly is guaranteed.

The development of Hangzhou Welfare Center has drawn attention from governments at all levels. National, provincial and municipal leaders have successively inspected the welfare center, guiding it into a more scientific development track. Also, the welfare center has cooperated with a number of universities and charity groups to establish student practice bases and organize volunteers to take care of old demented people in the center.

Initiated by the welfare center, Hangzhou Elderly Service Association was founded in 2014, which has been playing a positive role in further normalizing the development of elderly care service industry in Hangzhou.

Hangzhou Welfare Center has become a demonstrative base for training nursers and managers for nursing institutions throughout Zhejiang Province and has won the honorable titles of "National Model Nursing Institution for the Elderly", "Demonstrative Nursing Institution for the Elderly" and "Civilized Unit that Respects the Elderly".

杭州市妇女活动中心

舞台上身着旗袍的女子伴着音乐款款走来，她们优雅的仪态，曼妙的步履，充满神韵的表情，演绎着西子情怀，讲述着"杭州故事"，这是在中国丝绸博物馆举行的"杭州全球旗袍日"特色活动中的一场金秋旗袍演绎秀。杭州市妇女活动中心旗下的西子艺术社团旗袍社的队员作为特邀嘉宾，现场演绎了一场融合音乐与戏曲的古典旗袍秀。

杭州市妇女活动中心成立于1994年，是杭州市妇女联合会下属的一个公益性单位，旨在为中外女性朋友服务。活动中心内各类服务设施功能齐全，配有游泳馆、健身馆、美容美体馆、会议厅、培训教室、多功能艺体室等，集学习培训、健身休闲、文化交流等功能于一体，为广大女性搭建起公益性、综合性、国际化的女性成长服务平台。活动中心通过各类培训、联谊、咨询、援助、研究、公益等活动，满足杭州市广大女性在工作、生活等各方面的成长需求，是杭州市各界女性学习交流、开展活动、展现风采的重要窗口。

杭州市妇女活动中心塑造了西子系列服务品牌，通过西子女性大讲堂、西子艺术社团、西子女性学堂等服务载体，帮助和指导女性塑造美丽人生。

西子女性大讲堂以女性需求为导向，满足广大妇女多层次、多元化精神文化需求。主要举措是聘请杭州市各行业精英女性组成西子女性宣讲团，线上、线下同步开设精彩女性终身学习课程，宣传科学教子、健康身心、幸福婚姻及品质生活等方面的知识。特别是在主题活动中，结合家风家训宣传，连续开展"妈妈的

味道"母亲节活动,将中华优秀传统美德贯穿到家庭日常生活的点点滴滴中,融入每个家庭成员的一言一行中。

西子艺术社团自 2015 年成立至今,一直是杭城女性不断提升自我、完善自我的又一优质平台。西子艺术社团开设舞蹈、旗袍、合唱、摄影、舞台表演五个分社,不断讲授与时俱进的教学内容,开拓风格独特的教学模式,每年定期举办几次社团汇报展示,还组织参与各类赛事及公益活动,深受杭城各界女性欢迎。杭州市妇女活动中心西子艺术社团旗下的旗袍社成立于 2015 年,学员在这里学习旗袍礼仪、茶艺、形象管理、非遗文化体验等课程,她们身上有着独特的江南气韵与温婉典雅的气质,犹如"民间旗袍推广大使",演绎着精致大气的杭州新生活美学。

西子女性学堂以倡导品质生活为出发点,努力实现杭州女性思想观念、家庭教育方式、生活方式、情感样式的多重表达。西子女性学堂针对女性不同层次的需求,深入开展书法、国画、茶道、花艺、油画、素描、烘焙、妆容等培训,提高妇女的生活品位和文化素养。

杭州市妇女活动中心围绕杭州市妇联服务基层、服务妇女的工作宗旨，努力延伸服务触角。成立杭州市公益文艺宣传队以来，妇女中心发挥"全国排舞运动推广中心教学示范基地"的优势，定期开展集中培训和基层指导，以由点到线、由线到面的网格化管理开展文艺推广。全民健身，助推各县（市、区）妇联开展具有女性特色及需求的科学健身文艺活动，为杭州文明健康的城市形象添彩。

　　杭州市妇女活动中心还为杭城女企业家、初创期女创客、女大学生创业团队搭建交流平台，促进创业项目结对合作；中心努力优化服务家庭项目建设，通过幸福e家、"一缘一会"婚恋工作室、米豆亲子屋等载体，完善婚姻家庭服务平台建设，筑造幸福家庭的学堂；中心还通过心理咨询、法律解析、恋爱技能和科学婚恋观的指导，为杭城的年轻男女开展婚姻家庭指导课程服务，发布婚姻家庭指导信息，线上点击量超过五万；中心还在做"西子女性"网站、"西子女性"微信、"西子女性"新浪微博、"杭州发布"政务直通车共四个平台的信息编辑、报送、发布工作，网站信息资源更新近万篇，网站访问量逐年递增；中心"伊生活"亲子体验活动从"农耕文化""传统手工"着手，巧借社会力量，开展栽培、采摘、手工等亲子互动活动，"米豆"亲子屋指导家长掌握和树立与孩子有效沟通的技巧和正确的家庭教育理念。

　　杭州市妇女活动中心非常关心农民工子女的学习和生活，长期以来持续开展留守儿童夏令营活动，招募爱心志愿者赴淳安、建德，为当地的留守儿童带去关爱和温暖，点亮他们心灵的明灯。

Hangzhou Women's Activity Center

Women in cheongsam are coming towards us elegantly with graceful steps in the music. They are expressing the beauty of the West Lake and narrating the "story of Hangzhou" with romantic charm. This is a golden autumn cheongsam show which is held in China Silk Museum as a special event of "Hangzhou Global Cheongsam Day". As specially invited distinguished guests, the team members of Cheongsam Club of Xizi Art Association under Hangzhou Women's Activity Center present a live cheongsam show combining music with operas.

Established in 1994, Hangzhou Women's Activity Center is a public welfare unit under Hangzhou Women's Federation with the purpose of providing service for Chinese and foreign women. The activity center provides various service facilities and complete functions, including swimming pool, gyms, beauty and bodycare salon, conference hall, training room, multi-functional art and sports studios and so on. The center is integrated by learning and training, fitness and leisure, cultural exchanges and other functions and has built a non-profit, comprehensive and international female growth service platform for women. Through various training, fellowship activities, consultation, assistance, research and public welfare activities, it endeavors to meet women's demands for growth in work, life and all other aspects. It is an important window for

women from all circles to study and exchange, carry out activities and show their charm.

Hangzhou Women's Activity Center has built Xizi series service brands and helps women shape a beautiful life through Xizi Women's Lecture, Xizi Art Association, Xizi Women's School and other service carriers.

Oriented by women's demands, Xizi Women's Lecture aims to meet women's demands for multi-level and diverse spiritual pursuits. Its main initiative is to employ female elites from various industries in Hangzhou to form Xizi Women's Lecture Group to offer online and offline courses for women's lifelong study on how to be a wonderful woman, passing on knowledge on education of children scientifically, cultivation of sound body and mind, management of happy marriage and quality life. Especially, it promotes Chinese family disciplines with themed activities and has carried out "Taste of Mom-made Dishes" to celebrate the annual Mother's Day, which has successfully integrates time-honored Chinese traditional virtues into Chinese woman's everyday life.

Since its establishment in 2015, Xizi Art Association has become a good platform for women in Hangzhou to promote and elevate themselves. The association is subdivided into five branches such as dance, cheongsam, chorus, photography and stage performances, providing up-to-date teaching contents with distinctive teaching modes. Besides, it carries out all kinds of exhibitions each year at regular intervals, organizes and participates in various events and non-profiting activities, making it very popular among women of all circles in Hangzhou. For example, the Cheongsam Club under the Xizi Art Association is the very place for its members to learn about cheongsam etiquette, tea ceremony, image management and cultural experience of intangible heritages. With the grace and elegance that are unique to the women

in the southern regions of the Yangtze River, club members serve as "non-governmental ambassadors for the promotion of cheongsam", advocating new Hangzhou life aesthetics which features delicacy as well as inclusiveness.

To help women in Hangzhou to seek high quality life, Xizi Women's School has made endeavors to satify women's multiple appeals in ideology, family education, life style and emotional modes. For instance, the school provides courses like calligraphy, Chinese landscape painting, tea ceremony, flower arrangement, oil painting, sketch, baking, fashion and beauty training to upgrade women's taste of life and humanistic consciousness.

Second, focused on the tenet of serving the grassroots and serving women as required by Hangzhou Women's Federation, Hangzhou Women's Activity Center has been trying hard to extend its scope of service. Since the establishment of Hangzhou Non-profiting Art Publicity Team, the center has given play to its advantage as "the teaching demonstration base of National Line Dance Promotion Center" to carry out concentrated training and grassroots guidance on regular basis and to launch art promotion through grid management from dots-lines-planes. The fitness-for-all program has facilitated Women's Federation at regional, county and city-level to carry out scientific fitness and cultural activities with feminine characteristic based on women's demands and has made due contribution to building a civilized and healthy Hangzhou image.

Third, Hangzhou Women's Center also establishes exchange platforms for woman entrepreneurs, woman makers in start-up stage, and female college student entrepreneur teams to facilitate matchmaking and cooperation of venture projects. The center strives to optimize home service project construction, and depends on happy e-family, "Matchmaking" studio, Midou parent-child house and other carriers to improve the construction of marriage &

family service platform and build happy family schools. In addition, the center provides courses on marriage and family for young men and women, offering services such as psychological counseling, legal interpreting, interpersonal relationship developing, and love and marriage guiding. Its releases marriage and family information with online clicks of over 50,000. The center engages in the information editing, sending and releasing for 4 platforms, namely, "Xizi Women" website, WeChat, Sina Microblog, and "Hangzhou Release" government affair express. The website has published approximate ten thousand articles and the page view of the website has been increasing year by year. The E-life parent-child experience activities include "farming culture" and "traditional handwork" to do planting, picking and handworking by relying on social forces in the meantime. "Midou" Parent-Child House aides parents to form correct family education philosophy before conducting effective communication with children.

Hangzhou Women's Activity Center pays close attention to peasant workers' children's, study and life. For a long time, it has been setting up summer camps for left-behind children in Chun'an and Jiande counties in Zhejiang Province and recruiting volunteers to bring concern and warmth to them.

珠儿潭社区

珠儿潭附近的老百姓口口相传着一个美丽动人的故事。传说当年龙井有一条善良的老龙，一直保护着地方老百姓，深受大家爱戴。后来，狮峰来了一头凶恶的雄狮。这头雄狮到处作恶，百姓吃尽苦头。众人一合计，准备去找老龙来制服雄狮。面对苦难的百姓，老龙流下了伤心的泪水："我不是不愿意帮助你们除害，只是我太老了，可能斗不过这头狮子呀！"一个小伙子站出来说："难道没有别的办法了吗？"老龙说："如果能得到百花仙子的清香露，也许我还能试试。不过百花仙子住在千里外的森林里，路途遥远又艰险。"小伙子毫不犹豫地说："为了众乡亲的生命安全，我愿意去走一趟。"于是，老龙告诉了小伙子详细的路线。三个月后，小伙子历尽艰险终于取回了清香露。老龙把清香露擦抹在身上，顿时全身像披了一层铁甲。第二天，龙狮相斗，斗得昏天黑地，日月无光。狡猾的狮子眼看打不过老龙了，它使出奸计，钻进一个山洞。老龙追到洞口，遭狮子暗中偷袭，搏斗中老龙两只眼珠被狮子挖了出来。结果老龙的一只眼珠跌落在西湖边的玉泉，化为珍珠泉；另一只眼珠就落在了湖墅，成了珠儿潭。

珠儿潭位于京杭大运河边，是杭州拱墅区的一处景观。据珠儿潭附近居民回忆，早先珠儿潭里有一块石板，脚在其上踩踏便会冒出水珠，很像珍珠，为当地一大奇观，但此景观现已不复存在。还有人说，在 20 世纪 80 年代以前，珠儿潭的东南面有 4 只抱磴，磴高 0.45 米，磴面直径约为 1 米，两侧有虎头图案。后来因为附近修建高楼，建设地基打夯，所以潭被破坏。现在的珠儿潭已经被采取了保护措施，用长方形的围栏围住了。

今天的珠儿潭位于京杭大运河西岸，东起湖墅南路，南临草营巷，北至贾家弄，西到莫干山路。这一带已成了百姓安居乐业的社区。

珠儿潭社区蕴藏着丰富的历史文化遗产：东面运河沿岸有浙江省省级文物保护单位、著名的历史文化古迹富义仓码头和粮仓、始建于宋朝的香积寺石塔和香积寺庙等；北面为古巷贾家弄，因南宋丞相贾似道别墅在此而得名；南面是极具文化气息的信义坊商街。

珠儿潭社区紧邻运河，历史上的这一带有许多码头、仓储、米市、鱼市、小猪行、孵坊等，珠儿潭的居民一般也都从事这些繁重而简单的行业，他们生活在社会的底层，其居住条件都比较恶劣。许多家庭都居住在一种有天井的院子里，当时称为"墙门"。墙门里房屋狭小简陋，有些住房其实就是用木板简单地分割了一下，且板壁已裂缝斑斑，几代人拥挤在一起，毫无隐私可言。公共设施也严重缺乏。

改革开放后，珠儿潭成为杭州市第一批旧房改造项目的受益者。昔日破旧的墙门、狭小的天井、岌岌可危的木板房被清新、精致、人性化、时尚的公寓式住宅替代，居民的居住条件和周边环境得到极大的改善。今天的珠儿潭社区有 56 幢居民楼，2500 多户家庭，6000 多常住人口。在公寓式住宅连片的小区里有绿地、花草、树木、盆景、雕塑等景观，每个小区内都有小超市、商场、饮食店、小花园等便民设施和场所。此外，小区内医疗、保健、服务、警务系统一应俱全。在这温馨美好的居住环境中，珠儿潭的居民们有了安全感、亲切感、舒适感和文明感。

满足了物质生活的基本需求以后，珠儿潭的居民们安居乐业，享受着改革开放的红利，同时也进一步认识到追求精神生活质量的重要性。社区居民李秀英擅长十字绣花，她绣的花卉鸟兽栩栩如生，十分美丽，邻居们看得眼热心动，纷纷上门向她请教，李秀英索性在社区里办了个"李秀英绣坊"，组织社区内的退休人员、十字绣爱好者一起参与，她们经常一起绣花一起交流经验，久而久之这项传统十字绣工艺在社区内得到了发扬，被列为拱墅区的非物质文化遗产项目。

　　社区还有许多由居民自发组织的兴趣爱好者队伍,如舞蹈队、晨练队、书画队、歌咏队、腰鼓队、军乐队等,有近200人参与了这些活动,并有专业老师带领他们进行训练。每当重大节日庆典时期,社区广泛开展文艺会演、体育竞技、朗诵演讲、知识抢答、书画展览、老年健身表演等群众喜闻乐见的大型特色文化活动。

　　近年来,珠儿潭社区充分利用本地优越的公共基础设施、深厚的文化底蕴、优雅温馨的生活氛围,开创国际旅游文化社区,向海外友人展示当地丰富多彩的传统文化,以及当下代表中国寻常百姓家健康、愉快的品质生活。随着改革开放的深入,外国人对中国普通老百姓日常生活的兴趣越来越浓厚。珠儿潭社区曾经接待过许多批次的外国人到居民家来体验生活。比如,外国人与当地居民上午同去菜场买菜,学做杭州普通家常菜和小点心,品尝杭州传统名菜;下午参观居民作品展示厅,展品包括刺绣、摄影、书法、国画、绢制品等等,同时与居民进行座谈、交流。有时,社区还为来访客人提供现场书画表演、书画简单教学、太极拳教学、学说简单汉语等活动项目。

　　除此以外,客人还可以在周边进行小规模的运河文化体验,由当地居民陪同,对运河周围的历史、现状、古迹和文物保护情况等进行了解。社区还开辟了专门的游览线路:首先可以游览珠儿潭社区,然后参观江涨桥,再观赏乾隆坊御码头,考察反映漕运文化的富义仓,穿过大兜路历史文化街,参观始建于宋代的香积寺塔。有兴趣的话还可以乘坐运河水上巴士到拱宸桥码头,参观全国重点文物保护单位——拱宸桥及中国运河博物馆,最后乘坐水上巴士返回珠儿潭。

今天的珠儿潭,居民素质得到显著提高,社区服务功能日趋完善,已经是一个治安秩序良好、人际关系和谐、生活方式健康、居住环境舒适、社区管理有序、社区保障完善、生活服务方便的文明社区。假如你要了解杭州普通人家的日常生活,请务必到珠儿潭来。

Zhuer Pool Community

People living near the Zhuer Pool usually pass from mouth to mouth a touching story. Once upon a time, there lived in Longjing a warm-hearted old loong protecting the locals, who love and admire the dragon. Later, a ferocious lion came to the Lion Peak, committing evil deeds and making people suffer a lot. This led everyone to plan to come to the old loong to subdue the lion. In the face of this, the old loong shed tears of sadness: "I am not unwilling to help you to kill the lion, but I am too old to beat the lion!" A young man stood up and said: "Aren't there any ways?" The old loong then said: "If you can get the fragrance dew from the Flower Fairy, I can give it a try. But the Flower Fairy lives in a forest thousands of miles away, and the journey is long and dangerous." The young man said without hesitation: "For the safety of the folks, I am willing to take the trip." Hearing this, the old dragon told the young man the detailed route to the forest. Three months later, the young man finally took the fragrance dew back. The old loong wiped the fragrance all over his body, which turned out to be suits of armor. With this, the old dragon challenged the lion. The violent battle made the sun and the moon dull. Seeing that he was going to be defeated, the sly lion played a trick and hid in a cave. The old loong chased the lion all the way to the hole of the cave and was raided by the lion. The two eyeballs of the loong were dug out by the lion in the fight.

As a result, one eyeball of the old loong fell near the edge of the West Lake and turned into the Pearl Spring. The other fell at today's Hushu district, which became the Zhuer Pool.

Located on the edge of the Grand Canal, Zhuer Pool is a landscape of Gongshu District of Hangzhou. According to local residents, there used to be a stone slab in the pool. Whenever people set foot on the slab, there would be water drops coming out, which was a unique spectacle. Others say that before the 1980s, Zhuer Pool has 4 embracing rock steps in the southeast with a height of 0.45 meter and a diameter of 1 meter. There were tiger head patterns on both sides of the rock steps. Later, due to the construction of high buildings nearby, the pool was destroyed to some extent. The current Zhuer Pool is protected by a rectangular fence.

Today's Zhuer Pool is located on the west bank of the Grand Canal. It starts from Hushu South Road in the east, Caoying Lane in the south, Jiajianong in the north, and Moganshan Road in the west. This area has become a community where people live prosperous and contented lives.

The entire Zhuer Pool Community is rich in historical and cultural heritages. In the east is the Grand Canal along which there are Fuyi Cang Wharf and Granary, two cultural relic protection units at provincial level. The famous historical and cultural monuments of Xiangji Temple Stone Tower and Xiangji Temple, which were built in the Song Dynasty, are located there. In the north is the ancient Jiajianong Lane, which is named due to Jia Sidao, Prime minister of Southern Song Dynasty, whose villa was located here. In the south is the culturally-oriented Xinyifang Commercial Street.

Zhuer Pool Community is close to the Grand Canal where there used to have many docks, warehouses, rice markets, fish markets, piglets, and

incubators. Most residents of Zhuer Pool Community were engaged in blue-collar industries and remained at the bottom of society enduring harsh living conditions. At that time, many families lived in a courtyard with a patio, which was then called "wall door". The houses behind wall doors were simple and crude and were divided by wooden boards and cracked walls. Several generations lived together without any privacy. What's worse, there was a severe lack of public facilities.

After China's reform and opening-up, Zhuer Pool Community became the beneficiary of the first batch of old house renovation projects in Hangzhou. The dilapidated wall doors, the narrow patios, and the precarious wooden houses were replaced by fresh, refined, humanistic and fashionable apartment-style houses. The living conditions and surrounding environment of residents have been greatly improved. Today, Zhuer Pool Community has fifty-six residential buildings, with more than 2,500 households, and 6,000 permanent residents. In the apartment-style residential areas, there are wide-spread lawns, flowers, trees, bonsais, sculptures and other landscapes. Each residential area has convenient stores, shopping markets, restaurants, gardens and other convenient facilities. Medical care, health care, service, and police systems are also readily available. Different residential areas are linked together into the Zhuer Pool Community. Residents of Zhuer Pool enjoy a sense of security, intimacy, comfort and civilization here.

Now that the basic material needs have been satisfied, the residents of Zhuer Pool are aware of the importance of pursuing quality spiritual life. Li Xiuying, a resident of the community, is good at cross-stitching. Her cross-stitching of embroidered flowers and birds are so lively that her neighbors all go to ask for guidance. Seeing this, Li Xiuying set up a "Li Xiuying Embroidery Workshop" in the community to organize retired neighbors in the community to embroider and exchange experience together. Over time, this traditional cross-stitch craft has been carried forward in the community and is listed as an intangible cultural heritage project in Gongshu District.

Apart from the Embroidery Workshop, there are also many interest teams organized by residents themselves, such as dance team, morning exercise team, calligraphy and painting team, singing team, waist drum team, military band and so on. Nearly 200 people participate in these activities under the guidance of professional teachers. During grand festivals and celebrations, the community will carry out large-scale cultural events such as cultural performances, sports competitions, recitation speeches, knowledge rushing, calligraphy and painting exhibitions, and senior fitness performances.

In recent years, Zhuer Pool Community integrates local public infrastructures with profound cultural heritages to create elegant and warm living atmosphere and forge an international tourist and cultural community, which goes all out to present to the world colorful Chinese culture and the livelihood of Chinese households. With the deepening of reform and opening up policy, foreigners are becoming more and more interested in the daily life of ordinary Chinese people. Zhuer Pool Community has hosted many foreigners to experience Chinese way of living at residents' home. When home-staying, foreigners are invited by local residents to go to the markets in the morning, learn to make home-cooked dishes and various snacks, taste traditional Hangzhou cuisine. In the afternoon, they visit exhibition halls to enjoy residents' works such as embroidery, photography, calligraphy, Chinese painting, enamel products, and so on. In the meantime, they are invited by local residents to have casual meetings. Sometimes, the community offers live painting and calligraphy performances, interactive calligraphic teaching and learning, Tai Chi teaching, and Mandarin Chinese classes.

Moreover, foreign guests can experience the Grand Canal culture in the surrounding area of Zhuer Pool Community, accompanied by local residents who introduce to them the history, current situation, monuments and cultural relics about the Canal. For this, the community has designed two tour routes. In the first route, tourists can visit Zhuer Pool Community, Jiangzhang Bridge and Qianlongfang Imperial Wharf. In the second route, tourists can first pay a visit to Fuyi Warehouse that reflects water transportation culture in ancient China, then enjoy the Dadou Road historical and cultural street and finally visit the Tower of Xiangji Temple built in the Song Dynasty. If tourists are interested to know more about Zhuer Pool Community, they can take the canal water bus to the wharf of Gongchen Bridge, and visit Gongchen Bridge and China Canal Museum, the National Key Cultural Relics Protection Units.

The comprehensive quality of residents in Zhuer Pool Community has been significantly improved, and the community's service function is becoming better day by day. Zhuer Pool Community is a civilized one with stable social order, harmonious interpersonal relationship, healthy lifestyle, comfortable living environment, orderly community management, perfect community security, and convenient living service. If you would like to find out the daily life of ordinary people in Hangzhou, please come to Zhuer Pool Community.

小营·江南红巷

据《杭州市志》记载，小营巷在南宋时期是朝廷禁卫军金枪班和银枪班驻地。因为禁卫军小营部队驻扎在此，所以称为"小营巷"。又据记载，太平军第二次攻克杭州后，这里曾经是听王府的所在地（听王是太平天国的一种官位）。现在小营巷61号，即当时听王府的后面，仍然保留着太平天国时期的一幅壁画。1958年，毛主席曾经来到此地视察，小营巷因此名声大振，被誉为"江南第一名巷"。小营巷是毛主席视察过的唯一一个居委会。在这里，他亲切地与居民谈心，肯定并称赞了当地的卫生工作，从此把中国的爱国卫生运动推向了一个新的高潮。

小营巷始建于南宋，位于杭州上城区马市街与直大方伯巷之间，从东到西大约300米，是杭州城里一条普通的小巷。整个巷子小而幽静。小巷里的房子都有些年头了，但是周围环境却干干净净，加上见缝插针的绿化布置和充满生机的爬山虎，让人倍感小巷清幽整洁。

今天的小营·江南红巷已经成为一个红色旅游景区。整个景区风景优美，人文荟萃。毛主席视察小营巷纪念馆、国家爱国卫生运动纪念馆、中共杭州小组纪念馆、钱学森故居等众多历史底蕴深厚的纪念馆聚集在此，成为杭城一个旅游亮点。

毛主席视察小营巷纪念馆

1958 年 1 月 5 日,毛主席在赴杭州机场途中临时决定来小营巷视察卫生工作。他先后来到小营巷 61 号、56 号、42 号,察看了居民的卧室、厅堂、厨房、菜橱、水缸等,赞扬这里的卫生工作搞得不错。

新中国成立以前,小营巷垃圾成堆,污水存积,蚊蝇滋生,疾病流行。1946 年,一次麻疹流行,许多小孩病死。新中国成立以后,政府号召开展清洁卫生工作,特别是开展爱国卫生运动以来,小营巷铲平了"垃圾山",清除了"蚊蝇窝",改造了下水道,改进了防蚊设施,建立了卫生保洁制度,成立保健站,建立家庭病床,设立健康档案,实行计划免疫,从而再未发生疟疾、乙型脑炎、伤寒、白喉、麻疹等传染性疾病。同时,绿化美化环境,建立小营公园,办起了托儿所、红十字卫生站,推行文体活动,增强居民体质,保持文明卫生已成为群众的自觉行动。1954 年,小营巷居委会被评为上城区卫生模范单位,1956 年,又评上了杭州市卫生模范单位。

时光荏苒,60 年匆匆流逝,但是小营巷居民仍然怀念那令人激动的时刻,感恩毛主席深入基层、关心群众疾苦的爱民之心。人们在这里建立的毛主席视察小营巷纪念馆还原了毛主席视察小营巷的历史情景,表达了广大群众对伟人的缅怀之情,同时激发了人们建设健康社区的热情。

中共杭州小组纪念馆

1922 年 9 月初，浙江省第一个党的地方组织——中共杭州小组在皮市巷 3 号正式成立。当时，四位杭州党小组的骨干分子在这里秘密举行会议，成立了浙江省第一个中国共产党党小组。为了纪念这一伟大的历史事件，小营街道的居民们将这里——方谷园 3 号打造成了中共杭州小组纪念馆。

中共杭州小组纪念馆采用了传统和现代科技化手段相结合的展示手法生动再现了中共杭州党小组创建、发展、壮大以及最终形成燎原之势的全过程。

全馆由四个展厅组成。

第一展厅为潮起钱塘展厅。它采用了现代科技手段，生动再现了 1919 年五四运动时期，杭州省立第一师范学校的进步学生创建浙江省首部进步刊物《浙江新潮》时的情景。

第二展厅为星火钱塘展厅。展厅中的四位蜡像人物分别是杭州党小组的创始人徐梅坤，党小组组长于树德，党小组组员金佛庄、沈干城。成立党小组会议的场景则是根据老照片，按照 1 : 1 的比例进行了还原。

第三展厅为奔腾钱塘展厅。整个展厅采用了 116 块液晶显示屏进行无缝拼接，再现了钱塘江潮起的景象，预示着杭州党小组的力量如奔涌的钱塘江水般势不可挡。庭院里矗立着一座巨大的，以一面迎风飘展的党旗为背景的雕塑，以高浮雕的形式展示了杭州党小组的创始人及三位小组成员勇立潮头的伟岸形象。

第四展厅为今日钱塘展厅。它以灯箱、展板的形式展示了杭州自新中国成立后至今，在党的领导下，取得的各项傲人的成绩以及党和国家领导人对杭州发展的殷切关怀。

全国爱国卫生运动纪念馆

　　健康是促进人类全面发展的必要基础，是社会经济文化活动发展的基本条件。实现全民健康长寿，是国家强大、民族振兴的先决条件，也是全国各族人民的共同愿望。

　　中国首个爱国卫生运动纪念馆，坐落于杭州市区的小营巷。全国爱国卫生运动纪念馆以物品展示、浮雕刻画、多媒体展播等方式，展示了自 1952 年以来中国开展爱国卫生运动的历程，反映了爱国卫生运动在建设新中国的过程中做出的重要贡献。值得注意的是，纪念馆所在地杭州小营巷社区，正是中国爱国卫生运动发展的缩影之一。

爱国卫生运动纪念馆的参观内容分"爱国卫生运动的起源和兴起""爱国卫生运动的创新与发展""爱国卫生运动的推进与深化""爱国卫生运动的组织和保障"四个部分。在纪念馆古香古色的二层建筑中，陈列的物品均是由杭州市爱国卫生运动委员会办公室工作人员奔赴 20 多个省区市收集而来的相关史料和实物。

钱学森故居

有个中国人，20 世纪 30 年代在美国麻省理工学院航空系学习，后来转入加州理工学院航空系学习，在那里他先后获航空工程硕士学位和航空、数学博士学位。1938 年 7 月至 1955 年 8 月，他还先后任美国加州理工学院和麻省理工学院航空系副教授、教授，加州理工学院航空系教授和喷气推进中心主任等职。他还在美国从事火箭研究，参与国防机要，甚至一度在五角大楼上班。这个人就是中国航天事业的奠基人，享誉海内外的杰出科学家钱学森。

1949 年 10 月，当中华人民共和国宣告诞生的消息传到美国后，钱学森和夫人便商量着要早日回到祖国，为自己的国家效力。钱学森因此被美国当局怀疑为共产党人而遭到迫害。钱学森非常气愤，以此作为要求回国的理由。1950 年，钱学森准备上船回国时，被美国当局拦住并将他在特米那岛上拘禁了 14 天，直到加州理工学院送去 1.5 万美金的巨额保释金才将他释放。后来，海关又没收了他的行李，包括 800 公斤书籍和笔记本。

钱学森在美国受迫害的消息很快传到国内，国内科技界的朋友通过各种途径声援钱学森。1954 年，他写信给父亲的好朋友、时任全国人大常委会副委员长的陈叔通，请求中国政府帮助他回国。1955 年，经过周恩来总理在与美国外交谈判上的不懈努力，甚至包括释放 11 名在朝鲜战争中俘获的美军飞行员作为交换，1955 年 8 月 4 日，钱学森收到了美国当局允许他回国的通知。9 月 17 日，钱学森回国的愿望终于得以实现。这一天他携带妻子和儿女，踏上返回祖国的旅

途。1955 年 10 月 1 日清晨，钱学森一家终于回到了自己魂牵梦绕的祖国，回到了自己的故乡。由于钱学森的回国效力，中国导弹、原子弹的发射向前推进了至少 20 年。

钱学森是吴越国王钱镠的第 33 代世孙。钱氏家族在杭州是名门望族，钱氏家训中有"爱子莫如教子，教子读书是第一义"的训条。因此钱氏子孙人才辈出，在中国历史上赫赫有名的就有 100 多位，如钱学森、钱锺书、钱伟长、钱三强等。

钱学森故居前后三进，有厅堂、厢房、天井、过道等，占地 800 多平方米。2007 年曾进行过整体修缮，现故居通过"杭州之子""航天之父""情系故乡"三个单元再现了钱学森一家在杭州的生活场景。

Xiaoying · Jiangnan Red Lane

According to *Hangzhou Annals*, Xiaoying Lane was where the imperial guards (golden spear squad and silver squad) stationed in the Southern Song Dynasty. It was the place where the small camp force of the imperial guards stationed, hence it was named Xiaoying (literally means small camp) Lane. According to historical records, after the Taiping Army conquered Hangzhou for the second time, it was once the location of King Ting's Palace (King Ting was an official post in Taiping Heavenly Kingdom). Now, a fresco dating back to Taiping Heavenly Kingdom still remains at No. 61 Xiaoying Lane behind King Ting's Palace. As Chairman Mao visited here in 1958, Xiaoying Lane has become the most famous since then and has been dubbed as the "No. 1 Lane in the Southern Region of the Yangtze River". Xiaoying Lane was the only neighborhood committee of its kind ever inspected by Chairman Mao. Here, he chatted cordially with the residents and spoke highly of the local sanitary work. Since then, China's patriotic sanitation campaign has been pushed to a new climax.

Built in the Southern Song Dynasty, Xiaoying Lane is located between Mashi Street and Zhidafangbo Lane in Shangcheng District of Hangzhou. Extending about 300 meters from east to west, it is small and quiet. The houses along the lane are covered with greenbelts and creepers here and there, adding to the quietness and tidiness of the whole environment.

Today, Xiaoying Lane has become a red tourism block with beautiful scenery and rich cultural deposits. Memorial Hall Commemorating Chairman Mao's Inspection of Xiaoying Lane, National Patriotic Health Campaign Memorial Hall, Memorial Hall of CPC (the Communist Party of China) Hangzhou Team, Former Residence of Qian Xuesen (China's world-famous scientist in aerodynamics) and other deep-rooted historic halls are clustered here, making Xiaoying Lane a new tourism highlight in Hangzhou.

Memorial Hall Commemorating Chairman Mao's Inspection of Xiaoying Lane

On January 5th, 1958, Chairman Mao suddenly decided to inspect the sanitary work of Xiaoying Lane on his way to Hangzhou Airport. After successively inspecting the sites at No. 61, No. 56 and No. 42 Xiaoying Lane and the bedrooms, halls, kitchens, kitchen cabinets and water vats of the residents, he complimented that the sanitary work here was well-done.

Before the founding of People's Republic of China, Xiaoying Lane featured piles of garbage, hydrops of dirty water with multiplying mosquitoes and flies and prevalent diseases. In 1946, many children died of the outbreak of measles. After the founding of the People's Republic of China, the government called for carrying out sanitation and hygiene work. Especially, after the launch of patriotic sanitation campaign, the "garbage hills" were removed, the "mosquitoes and fly nests" were eliminated, the sewers were renovated and the mosquito protection facilities were improved. Also, the lane established a health and sanitation system, built health stations, set up family wards and made

health records. It conducted planned immunization so that malaria, Japanese encephalitis, typhoid, diphtheria, measles and other infectious diseases have been eliminated since then. At the same time, the lane beautified the living environment, established Xiaoying Park, built nursery and Red Cross health station, and carried out sports and cultural activities to enhance the physical fitness of the residents. The locals became conscious of being civilized and hygienic. In 1954, Xiaoying Lane Neighborhood Committee was considered as the Model Unit of Shangcheng District in Sanitation Work. In 1956, it was assessed as the Model Unit of Hangzhou City in Sanitation Work.

Time flies. Sixty years elapsed. Despite this, the residents of Xiaoying Lane remain grateful for Chairman Mao's concern on common people's lives. Hence, the Memorial Hall Commemorating Chairman Mao's Inspection of Xiaoying Lane was built to revivify the historic moment and further promote people's enthusiasm for health community building.

Memorial Hall of CPC Hangzhou Team

The first local CPC organization of Zhejiang Province—CPC Hangzhou Team was officially established at No. 3 Pishi Lane in early September of 1922. At that time, four key members of CPC Hangzhou Team secretly held meetings here and established the first CPC Party Team in Zhejiang Province. In memory of this great historic event, the residents of Xiaoying Sub-district built Memorial Hall of CPC Hangzhou Team at No.3 Fanggu Park.

The memorial hall adopts both traditional and modern technologies to vividly display the establishment, development, expansion and boom of CPC Hangzhou Team.

The hall is composed of four exhibition rooms.

The first exhibition room, named as the Room of Surging Qiantang, adopts modern technologies to vividly show the May 4th Movement in 1919 and the scenarios of the progressive students of Hangzhou Provincial No.1 Normal School founding the first progressive periodical *Zhejiang New Tide*.

The second exhibition room is the Room of Sparking Qiantang. The four wax statues in the room are Xu Meikun, the founder of CPC Hangzhou Team, Yu Shude, the Party team leader, Jin Fozhuang and Shen Gancheng, the Party Team members. The scenario of the foundation of Hangzhou Party Team was restored by a proportion of 1:1 according to the old photo.

The third exhibition room, the Room of Torrential Qiantang, diaplays the surging Qiantang River through the seamless spicing of 116 liquid-crystal display screens, indicating that the strength of the Hangzhou CPC Party Team is unstoppable like the surging wave of the Qiantang River. In the courtyard, there stands a high-relief sculpture of 4 stalwart images of the founder and three members of CPC Hangzhou Party Team standing on the tide, with the Party flag fluttering behind.

The fourth room, named as the Room of Qiantang Today, demonstrates with light boxes and display panels the outstanding achievements of Hangzhou under the leadership of the Communist Party since China's liberation as well as national leaders' ardent concern for the development of Hangzhou.

National Patriotic Health Campaign Memorial Hall

Health is the basis of promoting mankind's all-round development, the prerequisite for social, economic and cultural development, the condition for realizing citizen's good health, a strong country and national rejuvenation, as well as the common aspiration of all nationalities.

Located in Xiaoying Lane in downtown Hangzhou, the National Patriotic Health Campaign Memorial Hall was the first of its kind in China. Via article exhibition, relief carving and multi-media, the hall displays the progress of China in carrying out patriotic health campaign since 1952, and reflects the significant contribution of patriotic health campaign to people in China after 1949. It's worth noting that Hangzhou Xiaoying Lane Community, where the memorial hall is located, is one of the epitomes of the development of national patriotic health campaign in China.

The contents of the exhibition fall into four parts such as "Emergence and Rise of National Patriotic Health Campaign", "Innovation and Development of Patriotic Health Campaign", "Promotion and Deepening of Patriotic Health Campaign" and "Organization and Guarantee of Patriotic Health Campaign". The memorial hall is a two-storey antique building. All the articles on display in the building are relevant historical materials and real objects collected from more than 20 provinces by the staff of Hangzhou Patriotic Health Movement Committee Office.

Former Residence of Qian Xuesen

He is a Chinese. In 1930s, he studied in the Aviation Department of Massachusetts Institute of Technology and then studied at Aviation Department of California Institute of Technology, where he successively obtained the Master's degree for aeronautical engineering and the Doctoral Degree for aviation and mathematics. From July, 1938 to August, 1955, he was successively appointed the associate professor and professor of California Institute of Technology and Massachusetts Institute of Technology, the professor of the Aviation Department of California Institute of Technology and the director of Jet Propulsion Center. He was also engaged in rocket research and participated in America's national defense confidential projects and even worked at the Pentagon. The young man is Qian Xuesen, the founder of China's Aerospace Industry and an outstanding scientist enjoying global reputation.

In October, 1949, when the news of the foundation of the People's Republic of China reached the U.S.A., Qian Xuesen and his wife decided to go back to China as soon as possible to work for his own country. For this reason, U.S.A. authority suspected that he was a communist and started to persecute him. Qian Xuesen was angry and required to return China because of it. In 1950, when Qian Xuesen was about to board the ship back to China, he was stopped by U.S.A. authority and was constrained on the Terminal Island for 14 days. He was not released until California Institute of Technology bailed him with 15,000 US dollars. Later, the Customs confiscated his luggage, including 800-kilogram books and notebooks.

The news that Qian Xuesen was persecuted in the Unite States quickly reached China. Friends from scientific and technological circle expressed strong support for Qian Xuesen through various channels. In 1954, Qian wrote to a friend of his father, Chen Shutong, the Deputy Chairman of the Standing Committee of National People's Congress at that time, and asked the Chinese government to help him return to China. In 1955, the late Premier Zhou Enlai carried out a series of diplomatic negotiations with the U.S.A. government, including the release of 11 U.S.A. military pilots captured in Korea War. Thanks to Zhou's unremitting efforts, Qian Xuesen finally received the notice from U.S.A. authority allowing him to return to China on August 4th, 1955. On September 17th, he embarked on the journey back to China together with his wife and children. On October 1st, 1955, Qian Xuesen and his family finally

stepped onto the earth of China that he had been missing so much. Due to Qian's efforts, China launched missiles and atomic bombs at least 20 years in advance.

Qian Xuesen was the 33rd descendant of Qian Liu, the king of China's Wuyue State (907A.D.–978A.D.). Qian's Family is a notable family in Hangzhou. The family motto formulated by Qian Liu (also called King Qian) goes as follows: "The best way to love children is to educate them, and the best way to educate them is to teach them reading." Therefore, Qian's family has given birth to a galaxy of talented descendants, including more than one hundred famous celebrities in Chinese history, such as Qian Xuesen, Qian Zhongshu, Qian Weichang and Qian Sanqiang.

The Former Residence of Qian Xuesen is a three-hall building that includes halls, wing rooms, patios and aisles with a land area of more than 800 square meters. In 2007, the whole building was renovated with three units, namely, "Son of Hangzhou", "Father of Aerospace" and "Attachment to Hometown" ,showing the living scene of Qian Xuesen and his family in Hangzhou.

新华实验幼托园

新华实验幼托园隶属下城区教育局，是一所浙江省示范性幼儿园，浙江省教育厅贯彻《幼儿园教育指导纲要（试行）》实验园，杭州市甲级幼儿园，杭州市教委"托幼一体化"试点园。

杭州市新华实验幼托园的前身是杭州市新华路幼儿园，创办于 1951 年。它除了柳营幼儿部园区以外，还有两个园区：娃娃部、仙林幼儿部。新华实验幼托园的各园区实行"1+X"个性化运作："1"代表共性部分，即实施共性管理和共性课程；"X"代表特性部分，即特质管理和特色课程。

新华实验幼托园柳营幼儿部位于下城中心老城区，园舍建于 1990 年，是新华实验幼托园的大本营。柳营幼儿部科学教育的首要特色是"玩中学科学"。游戏是幼儿的天性，只有符合幼儿天性的教育，才会真正受到幼儿的欢迎。柳营幼儿部无论是集体教学活动的内容还是区域活动的内容，都充满了游戏精神，已形成以幼儿全面发展教育为基础，以"本色教育　童年慧玩"为特色的科学教育课程模式，培养幼儿"好奇、好问、好学、好动"的探究精神，启迪幼儿的智慧，突出营造"科学乐园"的园区文化氛围。教师还设计了各种科学小游戏，这些游戏让幼儿通过与材料的互动以及与同伴的互动，在区域活动中来体验和感受其中的科学原理。

园区在生态、绿色、健康环境方面保持鲜明的特色，并创设了有利于幼儿动手动脑、实践参与、大胆创造的自主活动空间，力图让园区的"每一面墙壁都说话"，

最大限度实现了"小空间大内涵"之目的，力争办成中心城区精品科技幼儿园。

在柳营幼儿部生活学习的三年里，孩子必须去体验的 10 件事分别是：1. 骑在爸爸肩上；2. 在雨中行走；3. 和父母下乡；4. 穿大人的衣物；5. 走"特别"的路；6. 参加一次今夜不回家活动；7. 在草坪上滚爬；8. 和父母一起看书；9. 至少参加一次幼儿园组织的亲子活动；10. 和父母一起种植一棵植物或饲养一只动物。

柳营幼儿部科学教育的另一个重要特色是"亲近自然"。这个园区里放眼望去都是绿意，到处都是植物，小朋友们仿佛置身一个雅致的绿色庭院。园区科学教育的一个重要目的就是培养幼儿亲近自然的态度与情感，让幼儿在直接接触自然、观察自然的活动中，逐步形成对大自然的积极情感。这里的每个班级都精心建造了自然角，选择不同的植物让孩子们参与种植与观察，及时传递自然的信息。

新华实验幼托园娃娃部位于下城区最南端，它在杭州市及浙江省率先启动"幼教低龄化"和"托幼一体化"的早教工程。娃娃部吸纳了先进的早教理念引领实践，以"开心、开口、开步、开窍"为发展目标，构建"幼托一体化"的课程体系。娃娃部在日托班机构设置的多元化、编班配备的合理化、环境创设的亲情化、营养保健的特色化、教育内容的生活化、教育对策的随机化等方面开展了实践研究。在办好日托班的同时，尝试举办灵活多样的亲子园，其已成为全省早教示范的窗口。娃娃部曾经设置过9个日托制托班，招收过最小的宝宝年龄仅仅18个月。2002年3月，幼托园以娃娃部为依托，创办了"园中园"——小脚丫亲子园，招收0～3岁社区散居婴幼儿。娃娃部园区也可以说是一所面向0～3岁婴幼儿开展早期教育的早教机构，是杭州市下城区孕育、实施、推广早教工程的种子园，也是市教委首批挂牌的"托幼一体化"试点园。随着园区的扩大，娃娃部搬迁到了新华路45号。

这个园区的特色就是绘本阅读。绘本阅读区可以说是娃娃部园区的"心脏"，里面拥有很多绘本。孩子们最喜欢坐在软软的坐垫上，拿起一本绘本，惬意地遨游在书籍的海洋之中。

园区里有许多经典的绘本形象，比如说《城里最漂亮的巨人》中的长颈鹿乔治、《你看起来好像很好吃》中的霸王龙。在这个园区每年举办的"亲子阅读节"系列活动中，孩子们和爸爸妈妈一起制作书签、绘本，进行亲子绘本剧的表演，在亲身参与的过程中感受绘本的魅力。这里墙面上展示的就是一些亲子自制绘本，这些特别的绘本背后记录了爸爸妈妈对孩子们浓浓的爱与美好的期待和孩子们七彩的成长故事。

新华实验幼托园仙林幼儿部是一所建造在老城区中心地段高档住宅小区内的幼儿园，是一所花园式幼儿园。园区充分依照地势开辟空间，因地制宜地对活动

室进行跃层、错层布局，使空间最大化合理利用。园区力争从早期阅读和儿童剧表演入手打造艺术特色，使幼儿园成为启迪幼儿艺术才能的摇篮。

2003年9月12日，十分关注并重视学前教育、时任浙江省委书记的习近平同志风尘仆仆地来到了浙江省示范性幼儿园之一的新华实验幼托园进行参观与视察。他通过深入一线来真切地了解杭州市学前教育发展的基本状况。习近平同志参观了幼托园的整体基础设施，还进入教室近距离地了解孩子们的生活。他详细地了解了幼托园的基本情况和"学前教育低龄化"的进展过程。他特别提到更小的孩子将如何教育，还提到开展早教的理论依据以及早教开发的价值。习近平同志还询问了老百姓最关注的入托问题和收费问题。习近平同志在参观的过程之中反复强调："启蒙教育很重要。"临走前，他又一次语重心长地说："这里是起步的教育，是很关键的一步。"习近平同志还鼓励园长和老师们："现在学前教育的创造空间很大，不要拘泥于传统的理论，理论本身也是在发展和探索过程中完善的。要进一步研究早期教育，成为全国的专家、世界的专家。"

近年来，幼托园实现了跨越式发展，取得的成绩令人瞩目。幼托园是省示范性幼儿园、省首批园本教研示范园、省教育厅贯彻《纲要》实验园、浙师大杭幼师实验园、省爱国卫生先进单位、市教委"托幼一体化"试点园、市教育科研先进单位、市"巾帼建功"示范岗、市首批社会资源国际旅游访问点，并且连续三年被评为下城区"平安校园"和"满意单位"。

Xinhua Experimental Nursery School

Xinhua Experimental Nursery School, within the jurisdiction of Department of Education in Xiacheng District, Hangzhou, is an exemplary kindergarten operating under the *Kindergarten Education Program Guidelines (For Trial Implementation)*, distributed by the Department of Education of Zhejiang Province. In addition, it is also rated as Class A kindergarten, and Pilot Nursery of "Intergration of Childcare" governed by Municipal Education Commission.

Founded in 1951, Hangzhou Xinhua Experimental Nursery School was formerly named as Hangzhou Xinhualu Kindergarten. The nursery school includes three parks: Liuying and Xianlin Kids Sections, and Infant Section. The parks develop unique operational mode "1+X": 1 means the parks operate common management and course; X, specific one.

As the home base of Xinhua Experimental Nursery School, Liuying Park, founded in 1990, is located in the old town of Xiacheng District. Its primary feature of science education is "learning science through playing" . Game playing is in tune with infant's nature, and only education that matches the nature can really be welcomed. Whether in collective teaching or in regional activities, Liuying Park is full of game spirit. Based on the infant comprehensive

development education, it has formed a science education curriculum model, featuring "nature education and smart play", cultivating the inquiry spirits of "being curious, inquisitive, studious, and active", enlightening children's wisdom, and highlighting the cultural atmosphere of the science park. The teachers also designed a variety of scientific games that allow young children to experience and feel the scientific principles in regional activities through interaction with materials and peers.

The park maintains distinctive features in ecology, green and healthy environment, creates an independent activity space that is conducive to infant's hands-on brains, practical participation, and bold creation, and strives to make the park "full use of every wall", maximizing "small space and big connotation", and to become a high-quality science and technology kindergarten in the central city.

The walls along staircases display the 10 activities that children are required to experience in their three-year life and study in Liuying Park. 1. Sit on daddy's shoulder. 2. Walk in the rain. 3. Go to countryside with parents. 4. Put on adult's clothes. 5. Take "special" road. 6. Participate in "Not Home-going Tonight" activity. 7. Roll on the lawn. 8. Read books with parents. 9. Participate in at least one parent-child activity organized by the nursery school. 10. Plant a tree or raise an animal together with parents.

The other major feature of its science education is "close to nature", where greenery was covered and the children seem to be in an elegant green courtyard. It aims to cultivate infant's attitudes and emotions close to nature, so that infant can gradually form positive emotions towards nature in the activities of direct contact and nature observation. Each class here has carefully constructed a natural corner, and has chosen different plants to allow children to participate in planting and observation, and to convey the information on nature in a timely manner.

The Infant Park, located at the southernmost end of Xiacheng District, has taken the lead in launching early childhood education projects in Hangzhou and Zhejiang Province with "early childhood education at a young age" and "integration of childcare". It absorbs early advanced education concepts and builds a curriculum system of "integration of childcare" with the four developmental goals of "to be delighted, to be communicative, to be active, and to be enlightened". The park has carried out practical research on the diversified daycare classes, rational class arrangement, cozy layout, specified nutrition and health care, daily educational content, and random educational measures. While running daycare classes, trying to hold flexible and diverse parent-child gardens has become a window for the demonstration of early education. The Infant Park has set up 9 daycare classes and founded the sub-park—Xiaojiaoya Parent-Children Park, which recruits 0-3 years old children from the community, where Xiacheng District government breeds, implements, and promotes early education projects. With the expansion of the park, it was relocated to No. 45 Xinhua Road.

The comic reading zone, as the characteristic and core of the park, provides a cozy and comfortable environment for children. They sat on soft cushions, picked up a picture book, swimming in the sea of books.

Many classic comic pictures were plastered on the walls, such as the giraffe George in "*The Most Beautiful Giant in the City*", and the tyrannosaurus Rex in "*You Look Like Delicious*". During the annual "Parent-Child Reading Festival", children and their parents make bookmarks, picture books, perform parent-child picture book shows, and feel the charm of picture books in the process of personal participation. Here are some parent-child self-made picture books displayed on the wall. These special picture books record the parents' strong

love and wonderful expectations for children and the colorful growth stories of them.

The Xianlin Park is built in a high-end residential area in the center of the old district. It is a garden-style kindergarten, and fully develops the space in accordance with the terrain. According to the local conditions, the activity rooms are layered and separated to maximize the use of space. The park strives to create artistic characteristics from early reading and children's play, becoming the cradle of inspiring children's artistic talents.

On September 12, 2003, Comrade Xi Jinping, who paid great attention to preschool education and was then the Secretary of the Zhejiang Provincial Party Committee, came to the Xinhua Experimental Nursery School, one of the demonstrative kindergartens in Zhejiang Province. He deeply understood the basic situation of the development of preschool education in Hangzhou by going deep into the grassroot level. Comrade Xi visited the overall infrastructure of the kindergarten, and also entered the classroom to get a closer look at the children's lives. He had a detailed understanding of the basic situation of kindergartens and the progress of "pre-school education at a low age". He specifically mentioned how younger children will be educated, and also mentioned the theoretical basis of early education and the value of early education development. Comrade Xi also inquired about the issues of entrustment and fees people were most concerned about. During the visit, he repeatedly emphasized: "Enlightenment education is very important." Before leaving, he said earnestly: "Here is the start of preschool education, a very important step." In addition, he encouraged the principal and teachers: "Don't stick to traditional theories. The theory itself is also perfected in development and exploration. We need to further study early education and become a national and even a world expert."

In recent years, kindergartens have achieved remarkably leapfrog development. It has been awarded many prizes—a provincial demonstration kindergarten, the first batch of garden-based teaching and research demonstration parks in Zhejiang Province, the provincial Education Department establishing the experimental nursery of the "*Kindergarten Education Program Guidelines (For Trial Implementation)*", Zhejiang Normal University Experimental Park of Kindergarten Teachers, the provincial patriotic health advanced unit, and the municipal education commission "childcare integration" pilot park, the city's advanced unit of education and scientific research, Hangzhou "the achievements of women" demonstration post, and Hangzhou's first batch of access points on social resources international tourism. Xinhua Experimental Nursery School has been rated as "Safe Park" and "Satisfactory Unit" in Xiacheng District for three consecutive years.

浙江旅游职业学院

浙江旅游职业学院是由文化和旅游部与浙江省人民政府共建的一所公办高等旅游院校。学院坐落于中国历史文化名城、风景旅游胜地——杭州，拥有萧山、千岛湖两大校区，共占地72万平方米，总建筑面积约27万平方米。两大校区分别与钱塘江、千岛湖交相辉映。萧山校区为国家AAAA级旅游景区，千岛湖校区依山傍湖，尽享AAAAA级景区资源，是理想的求知圣地。学院现为全国唯一一所旅游类国家示范性骨干高职院校，唯一一所国家旅游标准化示范院校，同时也是第一所通过联合国世界旅游组织旅游教育质量认证的旅游院校，教育部第一批教育信息化试点优秀单位。2017年被确定为"浙江省高职优质校建设单位"。

  浙江旅游职业学院是一所特色鲜明的旅游类高职院校。学院前身为 1983 年创建的浙江省旅游职工中等专业学校，2000 年升格为浙江旅游职业学院。学院设有酒店管理系、旅行社管理系、旅游规划系、外语系、艺术系、烹饪系、工商管理系、社科部、千岛湖国际酒店管理学院、国际教育学院、继续教育学院等 11 个系（部、院），开设有酒店管理、导游、烹调工艺与营养、空中乘务等 28 个与旅游业密切相关的专业，其中世界旅游组织旅游教育质量认证专业 11 个。

  浙江旅游职业学院秉承"励志、惟实、博爱、精致"的校训，致力于打造国际化的教育环境和高品质的教学团队。学院为浙江省国际化特色高校建设单位，是全省第一所具有招收外国留学生资格的高职院校。现设有非独立法人中外合作办学机构——中澳国际酒店管理学院，在莫斯科成立的中俄旅游学院是浙江高校在俄罗斯设立的第一所境外办学机构，其不断深化"开放多元、互融共建、文化

分享"的国际化办学机制。学院与瑞士洛桑酒店管理学院、澳大利亚威廉·安格理斯学院、英国谢菲尔德哈勒姆大学、意大利 ALMA 国际餐饮学院、俄罗斯国立旅游与服务大学、韩国顺天乡大学等 18 个国家和地区的 40 多所高校建立长期稳定的合作关系，与美国迪士尼公司、阿联酋迪拜豪华酒店集团、意大利歌诗达邮轮集团、日本温泉饭店等 80 余家全球顶尖旅游企业建立紧密合作关系，每年出国（境）留学（交流）、研修、实习、访问的学生占毕业生总数的 10% 以上，聘请外籍教师 30 余名。

浙江旅游职业学院致力于培养有社会之责任、敬业之精神、博爱之胸怀、国际之视野的旅游英才，努力建设成一所国内一流、国际知名的优质高职院校，着力打造成为旅游教育的"中国品牌"和"中国服务"人才培养的摇篮。

Tourism College of Zhejiang

Tourism College of Zhejiang (hereafter referred to as TCZJ) is a public college of higher tourism education under the administration of both the Ministry of Culture and Tourism of the People's Republic of China and the People's Government of Zhejiang Province. The college, located in the historic and cultural city of Hangzhou, boasts two campuses in Xiaoshan and Qiandao Lake, which added together, totals 1,080 *mu* (72 hectares). Xiaoshan Campus is a AAAA level tourist attraction, and Qiandao Lake Campus enjoys AAAAA level scenic resources, which are holy lands for knowledge. It is the only National Demonstrative Vocational College in the field of tourism education, the only National Demonstrative College in tourism standardization, and the first batch of Excellent Pilot Units in e-education. Moreover, among all the national tourism colleges in China, TCZJ was the first to pass TedQual (tourism education quality certification) by UNWTO in 2010, and is the first batch of excellent units for educational information pilots of the Ministry of Education. In 2017, it was labeled as one of the Construction Units of High-Quality Higher Vocational Schools in Zhejiang Province.

TCZJ is regarded as one of the key colleges in China specialized in tourism education. TCZJ was upgraded into a higher vocational college in 2000 from Zhejiang Vocational Secondary School for Tourism Employees, which was set up in 1983. It has 11 schools and departments, namely School of Hotel Management, Travel Service Management Department, Tourism Planning Department, Foreign Language Department, Art Department, Culinary Arts Department, Business Administration Department, Department of Public Courses, Qiandao Lake International Hotel Management School, School of International Education, and School of Continuing Education and so on. These schools and departments offer 28 tourism-related majors with Hotel Management, Tour Guiding, Culinary Arts and Nutrition, Tourist Attraction Development and Management, and In-Flight Service as flagship ones, among which as many as 11 professional majors have passed the UNWTO TedQual.

Adhering to the school motto of "Ambition, Pragmatism, Fraternity and Delicacy", TCZJ has been making endeavors to forge internationalized educational environment and quality teaching staff. For example, TCZJ is the Construction Unit of Universities in Zhejiang Province with Internationalized Characteristic and is the first higher vocational college in Zhejiang Province to enroll overseas students. It has under its supervision to set up the Sino-Australian International Hotel Management School which is located on Qiandao Lake campus as a non-separate legal entity. The Sino-Russian Tourism College which is set up in Moscow is the first overseas school-running institution in Zhejiang Province. In light of its principles of "opening, diversifying, integrating and sharing", TCZJ has established friendly and cooperative relations with 40 institutions of higher learning from 18 countries and regions, such as Ecole Hoteliere De Lausanne of Switzerland, William Angliss Institute of Australia, La Scuola Internazionale di Cucina Italiana, Russian State University of Tourism and Service, Soonchunhyang University of South Korea. It also cooperates with Walt Disney Company, Dubai Luxury Hotel Group, Costa Croiere S.p.A., Japanese Onsen Hotel and many world leading enterprises. Each year, 10% of the graduates engage themselves in studying, training, practicing and visiting abroad and more than 30 foreign experts are invited and many other countries to teach in TCZJ.

TCZJ, as one of the high-profile tourism colleges in China, has been cultivating tourism talents with dedication, social responsibility, philanthropic spirit and international vision. It is devoted to becoming a leading national and international key college specialized in tourism education, forging the cradle of talent training for "Chinese Brand" and "Chinese Service".